Studies in Writing & Rhetoric

Other Books in the Studies in Writing & Rhetoric Series

A Communion of Friendship

A Communion of Friendship

Literacy, Spiritual Practice, and
Women in Recovery

Beth Daniell

SOUTHERN ILLINOIS UNIVERSITY PRESS

Carbondale and Edwardsville

Publication partially funded by a subvention grant from The Conference on College Composition and Communication of the National Council of Teachers of English.

Quotations in chapter 3 from *One Day at a Time in Al-Anon* copyright © 1972 by Al-Anon Family Group Headquarters Inc. Reprinted by permission of Al-Anon Family Group Headquarters Inc.

Library of Congress Cataloging-in-Publication Data

Daniell, Beth, date.
    A communion of friendship : literacy, spiritual practice, and women in recovery / Beth Daniell.
        p. cm. — (Studies in writing & rhetoric)
    Includes bibliographical references (p.) and index.
    1. English language—Rhetoric—Study and teaching—United States. 2. Twelve-step programs—United States. 3. Women—Education—United States. 4. Female friendship—United States. 5. Adult education—United States. 6. Storytelling—Therapeutic use. 7. Literacy—United States. 8. Spiritual life. I. Title. II. Series.

    PE1405.U6 D36 2003
    808'.042'082—dc21
    ISBN 0-8093-2487-3 (alk. paper)   2002010566

Printed on recycled paper. ♻

This book is for my mother, who, listening to me, told me I had something to say.

Contents

Acknowledgments: The Social Nature of (My Own) Literacy

I am grateful to the Al-Anon women who offered me hours of audio-taped language from the initial and follow-up interviews. I am thankful that there were virtually no contradictions between the two sets of interviews. What these women generously shared turned out to be 161 single-spaced transcript pages, a trove of information on how literacy works in these women's spiritual lives. It was an honor to hear their stories and share their thoughts. In chapter 1, "A Dais for My Words," I discuss in more detail my relationship with these remarkable women, and in appendix B, "An Essay on Research and Telling the Truth," I talk about the problems in bringing to book form the rich information they shared with me.

In addition, in the years since the interviews, the Al-Anon women have discussed with me by phone and by mail what I have written about them. They have read conference papers, journal articles, and the chapters of this book. Catherine corrected typos and linguistic infelicities in drafts of chapters 1, 2, 3, and 4. I am grateful for the women's continued interest in this project.

Portions of this book have appeared earlier in different form. Portions of the introduction and chapters 4 and 5 were previously published as "Narratives of Literacy: Connecting Composition to Culture," *College Composition and Communication* 50 ([1999]: 393–410). Copyright © 1999 by the National Council of Teachers of English. Reprinted with permission. Portions of chapter 1 and appendix B were published as "The Will to Truth: Dilemmas in Writing Research," *Against the Grain: A Volume in Honor of Maxine Hairston*, ed. David Jolliffe, Michael Keene, Mary Trachsel, and Ralph Voss (Cresskill, NJ: Hampton, 2002, 185–95). Parts of chapter 2 were previously published as "Composing (as) Power," *College Composition and Communication* 45 ([1994]: 238–46); and Response, *College Composition and Communication* 46 [1995]: 284–88). Copyright xii **Acknowledgments**

© 1994, 1995 by the National Council of Teachers of English. Reprinted with permission. An earlier, brief version of chapter 3 was published as "'A Communion of Friendship': Literacy, Orality, Voice, and Self Outside the Academy," *Literacy Networks* 2 ([May 1996]: 55–63). Thanks to all of the previous publishers for permission to reprint.

Al-Anon Family Groups and Alcoholics Anonymous World Services have graciously given permission to quote from their publications, and I am thankful. I want to acknowledge as well the good both organizations do.

Within the Conference on College Composition and Communication (CCCC), a rich circle of scholars who work on literacy and especially on the literate practices of real people has nourished my thinking: Ann Berthoff, Deborah Brandt, JoAnn Campbell, Kim Donehower, Anne Gere, Juan Guerra, Kristine Hansen, James Moffett, Peter Mortensen, Beverly Moss, Jan Swearingen, Mary Trachsel, and Keith Walters.

I acknowledge as well the influence and assistance of many others. Long ago, Lester Faigley and James Sledd introduced me to literacy theory and research. My first partners in literacy were fellow graduate students Keith Walters and Mary Trachsel. When I first began thinking about this project, Susan Hilligoss recommended Carol Christ's *Diving Deep and Surfacing*, whose words, quoted in my introduction, have given me reason to continue. Martin Jacobi discussed Kenneth Burke with me, and Kevin Dettmar introduced me to Jean-François Lyotard. Mara Holt referred me to Dorothy E. Smith's work on research, truth, and postmodernism.

Art Young has read various versions along the way and offered immensely valuable suggestions on chapters 2 and 3. More recently, both Art and Keith, going beyond the call of duty, have read the completed manuscript, commenting intelligently, tactfully, and productively. Robert Brooke, editor of Studies in Writing & Rhetoric (SWR), has worked with me on this project, offering excellent advice and infinite patience. For SWR, Richard Miller, Juan Guerra, Beverly Moss, Rochelle Harris, Maria Monteperto, and Ginny Crisco read earlier versions of the manuscript, pointing out strengths and weaknesses and at the same time offering encouragement. Joe Harris, Kevin Dettmar, and various anonymous readers for *CCC* and *SWR* have pushed me to consider other questions and to clarify muddy language. I thank all these readers and the staff at Southern Illinois University Press. Infelicities remaining are my own.

The interview research was funded by Provost's Research Grants from Clemson University; chapter 2 was completed and chapter 3 begun during a sabbatical semester. Various chairs and deans have allowed me to schedule administrative duties so that some time was available each week to read and write. I am grateful for help from a number of research assistants over the years: Shelley Sharp, Heather Sehmel, Vickie Neapolitan, Mattio Valentino, Rebecca Barnett, Brett Lamb, and James Romesburg. Students in my literacy seminars and rhetoric classes have contributed to this work in uncountable ways.

I remember, as Tillie Olsen has admonished us to do, the generations of women who have been—and are in some places still—denied literacy in any form and those women nearer to us whose literacy has been restricted: "How many of us who are writers have mothers, grandmothers, of limited education; awkward, not at home, with the written word, however eloquent they may have been with the spoken one? Born a generation or two before, we might have been they" (184).

A Communion of Friendship

Introduction

Women's Stories Have Not Been Told

This book is about women's literacy. More specifically, it is about the literacies used by one group of women in their spiritual practice. It is not, then, about the literacy of abstract, theoretical women. It is not about the literacy of women in general, or of American women, or of white women, or even of women who are or have been married to alcoholics—though the women I write about fall into those categories. Because it is about the literacy of real women who live in our culture, this book does not report on a wide variety of literacies. The kinds of reading and writing women do are still restricted, more these days—we are thankful—by convention than by statute. Thus this book is mostly about private and personal uses of literacy, practices allowed to women because such forms of reading and writing have typically been regarded as less important than the more visible and public literacies used by men. But for the women who talked with me, and for perhaps other women and men as well, private literate practice is of the utmost importance because it aids the development and empowerment of the self.

According to John Trimbur, examination of "how individuals and groups engage in self-formation, not as an autonomous activity but as a practice of everyday life" enriches other work in composition studies (130–31). The research I present here attempts to do precisely that: to show how six women use reading and writing to re-form themselves. The Mountain City women engage in literate practices in order to grow spiritually and emotionally, to live more self-aware lives, to attain personal power, to find or make meaning for themselves, to create community. Among the women I interviewed, both reading and writing occur in the context of oral teachings and conversations, which act as both generative and hermeneutic tools. Presenting the voices of these women, I argue against the view that literacy can be decontextualized or can be separated from orality. In the lives of the women who talked to me, reading and writing and talking are intertwined, embedded in each other. There is no text without talk—and very little talk without texts. I hope that my work can serve, then, as corrective to what I have argued elsewhere is the reductionism of modernist narratives of literacy ("Narratives"), to academic myths about reading and writing including the one that says that the terms *spiritual* and *emotional* are not legitimate categories for discussions of literacy, and to a research tradition that has assumed, until recently, that women's lives were not important enough to study or write about.

The women whose literacy I write about are not composites. They are quite real and wonderfully human. The six of them live in or near the town where I had my first full-time university position, a place I call Mountain City because of its location in the Appalachian Mountains, though I hasten to add, as I have learned I must, that Mountain City and the people who live there are not Southern. (Because the Appalachian chain runs from southern Quebec to northern Alabama, Appalachia and the South are not synonymous terms, though certainly the two regions overlap in places). When I interviewed these women in 1990, 1991, and 1992, they reported on literate practices that some of them had been engaged in for as long as ten years. In this book I call these women Catherine, Jennifer, Jill, Judy, Lilly, and Tommie. When I began this project, I thought of them as individuals—and certainly they are, with very different personalities and backgrounds—but as I studied the transcripts of the interviews, I realized that they were as well a tightly knit community created for the most part through their literate and spiritual practices.

Considering the differences in backgrounds, the disparity of their husbands' jobs and incomes, the wide variety of their children's ages, and the size of Mountain City, it is doubtful these women would ordinarily have known one another; certainly they would not have become friends (see Allan, esp. 20–24). But they were married to men who are alcoholics. The women who talked to me about their literacy came to know one another through Al-Anon, a self-help organization for families and friends of alcoholics. Founded in the 1950s and patterned after Alcoholics Anonymous, Al-Anon defines itself as a spiritual program. The literacy examined in this book isn't, then, just any reading and writing, but the reading and writing the Mountain City women did and do in pursuit of what Al-Anon calls "a spiritual awakening." It is through literacy in this spiritual context, I argue, that the women became a community, or, as Lilly puts it, a "communion of friendship."

Literacy

In this book the term *literacy* does not mean merely decoding or encoding sounds; nor is it a synonym for education, a use of the term altogether too general to be helpful. Rather, this book is about literacy as "the realized capacity to construct and construe in graphic form representations of our recognitions" (Berthoff 142). This book, in other words, is about reading and writing meaningfully. While this book certainly has to do with taking information from texts or creating texts that include information, it is, more precisely, about literacy as social practice. That is, I look at the literacy of the Mountain City women in both senses of the word *practice*—as repeated action and as an action that is engaged in in order to improve or reach a higher state. I have learned to think of literacy as event, as action, as ideological, as local, as gendered, as complying with the structures of society, and as resisting those structures.

Recently, in an article called "Narratives of Literacy: Connecting Composition to Culture," I used Jean-François Lyotard's notion of modernist "grand narratives" to categorize the literacy-orality theory of humanist scholars like Jack Goody and Ian Watt, Eric Havelock, David Olson, and Walter Ong as a *narrative of cognition* and Paulo Freire's thinking on literacy as a *narrative of liberty.* In one of theses stories, literacy acts "autonomously"—Brian Street's word (*Literacy*)—to make us smarter; in the other, it makes us free by endowing us with critical thinking (see Bizzell, introduction). Both narratives, I argue, overstate their claims. In addition, in composition and rhetoric, proponents of each narrative have often failed to see the political and ideological baggage that these perspectives carry with them. In the eighties and nineties, cross-cultural, ethnographic, and Marxist studies combined with poststructuralist theories of language and self, feminism, cultural studies, and ethnic studies to produce the next generation of research into literacy, which, if we continue with Lyotard's terms, might be called postmodern "little narratives."

Employing a variety of research methods, coming from several academic traditions, and, not unexpectedly, ranging in quality, the little narratives help us "gaze in wonderment at the diversity of discursive [and literate] species, just as we do at the diversity of plant or animal species" (Lyotard 26). The little narratives examine literacy in particular local settings, the best of them presenting the contradictions and complexities of specific literate practices. While such little narratives of literacy offer valuable insights into literate behaviors and while they may theorize on these social practices, they seldom make statements that claim to be valid for literate persons in general or literate cultures in general. These studies assume, rather, that literacy is multiple, contextual, and ideological. In addition, those taking a cultural studies approach display distrust of narratives in which one group becomes powerful because of the adoption of a supposedly neutral technology of literacy. These analyses often show the complexity in actual practice of the relationship of orality and literacy, or spoken and written language.

Interestingly, many of the little narratives—but certainly not all—are written by women, and many of their subjects—but not all—are women. One of the earliest was Janice Radway's 1984 *Reading the Romance: Women, Patriarchy and Popular Literature,* an examination of how middle-class women read romance novels. Allowing her subjects to speak for themselves, Radway captures the contradiction between the ideological content of the romance books and the ideological function of the women taking time away from their roles as caregivers to read. Linda Brodkey's "On the Subject of Class and Gender in 'The Literacy Letters,'" Jennifer Horsman's *Something in My Mind Besides the Everyday,* and Anne Gere's "Kitchen

Tables and Rented Rooms: The Extracurriculum of Composition"
open windows into the literacy—and lives—of poor and working-
class women, often revealing the gap between these women and the
middle-class teachers and social workers who try to help them.
Gere's *Intimate Practices: Literacy and Cultural Work in U.S. Women's
Clubs* shows how the reading and writing in women's clubs of the
late-nineteenth and early-twentieth centuries helped create community and identity for these women, while connecting them to the
wider political and cultural issues of their times and providing them
a means for speaking for the interests of their ethnic, racial, and
religious groups. Also falling into this category are two recent studies of the literacy of girls, Margaret J. Finders's *Just Girls: Hidden
Literacies and Life in Junior High* and Meredith Cherland's *Private
Practices: Girls Reading Fiction and Constructing Identity.*

Deborah Brandt's recent interviews with a number of adults
of varying ages and backgrounds tease out the ambiguities and poi-
gnancies of acquiring and using literacy in America in the twentieth
century ("Accumulating"; "Remembering"; "Sponsors"). Though
Brandt shows how literacy has allowed for social mobility or contributed to the construction of identity, her work also takes into account the losses that have been, and are still, part of the price of
literacy. Similarly, Kim Donehower's research focuses on the often contradictory experiences of literacy acquisition in a mountain
community in western North Carolina. Historical studies like Gere's
Intimate Practices and Janet Duitsman Cornelius's *"When I Can Read
My Title Clear": Literacy, Slavery, and Religion in the Antebellum
South,* which examines rich traditions of literacy among African
Americans during slavery, remind us to be cautious with statements
about the historical relations of literacy (and orality), on the one
hand, and race, class, or gender, on the other. Such works inform us
that the dominant tradition is not the only one, that countertradi-
tions run alongside, that history is usually more complex than it is
presented.

Another group of little narratives examines the relations of literacy and religion or spirituality: for example, Beverly Moss's study
of literacy in three African American churches in Chicago; Andrea

Fishman's work on reading and writing in an Amish community; Cushla Kapitzke's analysis of the literate practices of a Seventh-Day Adventist congregation in Australia; and my examination of literacy among women in Al-Anon. While these researches support the assertion of historical studies that religion and literacy are inextricably intertwined in many societies, they point as well to the variety this relationship can take (Goody, introduction; Resnick and Resnick).

The little narratives offer a variety images of what it means to be or to become literate in this culture and its various subcultures. They show people reading and writing for specific purposes: for entertainment, for personal growth, for identity formation, for community, for privacy, as well as for problem solving, for receiving and transmitting information, for economic advancement, for political empowerment for oneself or one's group. Varying in their overt politicization, the little narratives show that the modernist promise of literacy—economic security, upward mobility, political freedom, intellectual achievement, middle-class values, personal fulfillment—is inequitably fulfilled. But they also show that some people use literacy to make their lives more meaningful, no matter what their economic and political circumstances are.

The little narratives of literacy situate writing as part of everyday life, moving research into what Gere has called "the extracurriculum of composition." This body of research responds to the questions postprocess composition studies should be concerned with: Why and how do people in our culture read and write when they are not compelled to by the state, what are the functions and forms of these various literacies, what do these practices mean to the participants, to college students, to composition studies, and to the wider culture, and how do those meanings vary from this group to that? The partial answers provided by the little narratives of literacy offer a richer perspective than we once had on the writing our students may do outside our classrooms or the writing they may be called to do. The little narratives underscore that we teach actual not abstract students to write, not just for the next professor but for life in the culture.

In addition, because the little narratives take for granted literacy as multiple, contextual, and local, they often focus on the confluence of literacy with race, class, and gender, emphasizing the plurality of literacies and the differences among them. Like other postmodern work in composition as well as other disciplines, the little narratives are marked by a tension between Foucauldian determinism and human agency, showing the power of institutions to control people by controlling their literacy and the power of individuals and groups to use literacy to act either in concert with or in opposition to this power. As the little narratives make clear, literacy can oppress or resist or liberate, and the best of these studies present the simultaneity of these ideological contradictions. Taken together, the little narratives present, not one Truth but rather many truths about literacy.

Spirituality

The little narrative of literacy I present in this book is about the local, specific literacy practices of actual women engaged in a particular spiritual program. The Mountain City women *practice* their spirituality in both senses—repeating an action and engaging in an action for improvement—within in the context of Al-Anon. As readers will see in chapter 5, the idea that this book is about spirituality makes me a little nervous. Throughout this book, I define and redefine the terms *spiritual* and *spirituality*, but let me begin with simply this: consciousness of a spirit, or the spirit, of gods, or a God, of some force for good beyond the material world, of what people in Alcoholics Anonymous and Al-Anon call a higher power. It is the sense of being part of something bigger than oneself, of being connected to something higher than one's quotidian concerns. When asked for a definition of spirituality, the Mountain City women say, "Everything, hon, just everything" but also "confidence" and "belief in myself," connecting personal growth and emotional health with spiritual progress, notions of spirituality shaped by both AA and Al-Anon.

A Communion of Friendship is not about seances or new-age

philosophies or fundamentalism or even mainstream Christianity. It is not about religion as the term is typically used. Both Al-Anon and Alcoholics Anonymous claim to be spiritual but not religious programs. Though an anthropologist would likely classify both organizations as a religion and a sociologist or religious historian would see AA and Al-Anon as "a new religious movement" (Lester), I maintain in this book the AA–Al-Anon distinction. Some members of AA or Al-Anon explain the difference by joking that religion is for those who are afraid of hell, while spirituality is for those who have been there. A recent book explains that the postmodern age has revived the term *spirituality* to stand as contrast to both materialism and organized religion (Kurtz and Ketcham 24), and I use the term in that way as well.

According to tradition and published accounts (Kurtz; Jensen; Robertson), Alcoholics Anonymous began in 1935 when two alcoholics, Bill W., a stockbroker from New York, and Dr. Bob, a physician from Akron, Ohio, met in Akron. Each had separately become involved with the Oxford Group, an interdenominational organization that attempted to practice the principles of first-century Christianity (see Kurtz on the provenance of the Oxford Group, not to be confused with the Oxford Movement). As Dr. Bob and Bill W. kept each other sober through the confession and prayer recommended by the Oxfordians, they began, as well, to seek out other alcoholics with whom to share the news of their own salvation from alcoholism. Amazingly, for the first time in their lives, they each stayed sober. In 1939, when the *fellowship,* as it is called, had come to include about a hundred men (the earliest members were all men) in Ohio and in and around New York City, the organization published its first book, *Alcoholics Anonymous,* familiarly known as the Big Book, because the first edition was printed on thick paper in order to lend the publication some weight (Jensen 42).

In explaining how their program of finding and maintaining sobriety worked, Bill W., the chief author, divided the six spiritual practices of the Oxford Group into more discrete steps, listing for the first time the "Twelve Steps of Alcoholics Anonymous" (see appendix A for Al-Anon's Twelve Steps, adapted from AA). The steps, whether six or twelve, include admission of one's problem or sin, surrender, a personal inventory, confession to "God, ourselves, and another human being," reparations to those who have been harmed, ongoing prayer, meditation, and "sharing the message" with others. In both AA and Al-Anon, practice of the Twelve Steps is supposed to bring a spiritual awakening; the Twelfth Step of both groups begins, "Having had a spiritual awakening as a result of these Steps, . . . "

In the 1950s, AA members' wives who had been meeting informally in various locations around the country came together to found Al-Anon. The wives understood that alcoholism was a family disease and had discovered as well that when they themselves *worked the steps*, their lives, too, became better. Borrowing directly from the AA program, these women, including Lois W., Bill W.'s wife, and her friend, Anne B., adapted the AA program so that family members could use these same principles to repair the damage of living with an alcoholic. Wives and other family members sought not sobriety from drinking, but rather serenity, release from their confused and distressed thinking.

Early on, each program had begun to accept members of the other sex, women in AA and men in Al-Anon, though even now men still predominate in AA and women in Al-Anon. In my ten-years' experience in Al-Anon in five states, men were relatively rare in regular Al-Anon meetings, especially in smaller towns, but showed up in significant minorities in Al-Anon groups serving chiefly adult children of alcoholics. "Adult children" meetings began in the late seventies and early eighties, when many Baby Boomers came to *the program* for help with their own addictions or those of a spouse or other intimate and then began to realize that they had grown up in families affected by alcoholism. Not all meetings of adult children of alcoholics are Al-Anon meetings, but some Al-Anon meetings focus particularly on adult children. As the Boomers came to "the program"—by which term is meant going to meetings, practicing the steps, and engaging in the other customs of a Twelve-Step organization—the language of the program began to move into the popular culture, sometimes as the source of parody and jokes on such television shows as "Saturday Night Live" and other times as the negative focus of critics of pop culture such as Wendy Kaminer.

The women I interviewed talk a great deal about the steps, often just by number: "In Step Three, you get your power," Tommie declares without explaining Step Three ("Made a decision to turn our will and our lives over to the care of God *as we understood Him*"). In the text, I usually insert the relevant reference, but readers may find the complete list helpful in following the conversations in chapters 2 and 3; the Twelve Steps of Al-Anon are in appendix A. Other AA and Al-Anon, or program, language might trip a reader unfamiliar with these organizations: A *newcomer* is encouraged to find a *sponsor*—a combination spiritual mentor and confidante, usually a veteran member, often an *oldtimer,* someone who has practiced program principles for several years. A sponsor offers advice and guidance on working the steps and on rare occasions directives on personal decisions. Lilly serves as sponsor to some of the other women who talked to me.

When a person has been *in the program* for enough time to feel comfortable working the steps, he or she might offer, typically at the behest of her or his sponsor, a testimony, that is to say, the story of his or her life before the program and how she or he *got better* by working the steps. Included in this discourse in Al-Anon are comments about one's attainment of *serenity* and *courage,* two attributes specifically sought in the Serenity Prayer ("God grant me the serenity to accept the things I cannot change, courage to change the things I can, and wisdom to know the difference."). In Texas, where I first began attending Al-Anon meetings, this testimony was called *telling your story,* but in Mountain City it is called *giving a lead.* In both places, the testimony signified another level of membership (see Jensen for a Bakhtinian analysis of AA storytelling). In addition to such *speaker meetings,* there are *step meetings,* which focus on a different step at each meeting, and *discussion meetings,* which center on a topic, such as serenity, detachment, prayer, or surrender, chosen by the chair. *Open meetings* are for program members, but the public is welcome; *closed meetings* include only members of the particular program, with no visitors.

Language in both AA and Al-Anon relies on *slogans*—such statements as "One day at a time," "Let go and let God," "Keep it simple," and "Easy does it." Later in this book, I recount Lilly's explicit remarks about the slogans, but readers should be aware that the women incorporate them into their speech almost unconsciously. In these cases, I have tried when possible to include the women's elaboration of the concept or to present my own gloss on their remarks, but readers should be aware that the slogans are shorthand for shared experience and are often spoken with some degree of irony because insiders know how difficult these directives are to achieve. One Al-Anon member explains, "Because it was simple, I thought it was easy."

Central to the practice of both AA and Al-Anon are reading and writing. Indeed, middle-class assumptions about the value of literacy seem to have been part of the program since its beginnings. Bill W. and Dr. Bob were relatively well educated and early on required writing and reading of their followers. In Al-Anon meetings and in private conversation, members are regularly exhorted to "read the literature." Formal meetings begin with various members reading aloud the Suggested Welcome, the Twelve Steps, the Twelve Traditions, and the day's page in a book entitled *One Day at a Time in Al-Anon,* commonly referred to as "the ODAT" (pronounced *OH-dat*). In step meetings, the reading generally comes from *Al-Anon's Twelve Steps and Twelve Traditions* (called "the Al-Anon Twelve and Twelve" to distinguish it from its AA exemplar). Discussion often consists of sharing interpretations of a text from one of these books or from some other Al-Anon publication. Only literature approved by the World Service Conference of Al-Anon Family Groups is supposed to be read in meetings. In some groups, anything except the most casual mention of texts besides conference-approved literature (CAL) is subtly or explicitly proscribed, including even AA literature. This is not to say that Al-Anon members don't read and discuss other sorts of texts; indeed they do, as I describe in chapter 3. What the CAL policy means is that, while members are free to engage in all sorts of therapies or subscribe to all kinds of beliefs, examples of outside literature are not to be used as the basis for the talk that goes on at meetings.

The Fourth Step—"Made a searching and fearless moral inventory of ourselves"—is almost universally taken to mean a *written* inventory; in fact, the Al-Anon publication *Blueprint for Progress* is a workbook to help in the Fourth Step inventory and includes much white space for writing responses to the questions and exercises. The Eighth Step is usually understood as making a *written* "list of all persons we had harmed." While literate practices are an integral part of the program, reading and writing in Al-Anon are governed, I submit, by its oral teachings. George Jensen reaches a similar conclusion about the importance of the oral tradition in generating AA testimonies.

Connections

For most readers of the Studies in Writing & Rhetoric series, a connection between rhetoric and literacy is apparent. The inclusion of spirituality into the mix, however, may bring pause. When I first began this project, I received a number of puzzled looks from CCCC colleagues. These days, spirituality as a topic may not be quite so disconcerting to academics, but relations among rhetoric, literacy, and spirituality merit some comment here. The connection is power.

Rhetoric is always about—among other things, like pedagogy, beauty, knowledge, reason, and so forth—the power of language, not only to get work done in the world but also to control or influence others. In "Encomium of Helen," the Sophist Gorgias compares the effect of speech on the soul to the effect of drugs on the body: "Speech is a powerful lord . . . it can stop fear and banish grief and create joy and nurture pity" (52). In the *Antidosis*, Isocrates asserts that the power to persuade by means of language has allowed human beings to produce laws and arts, which in turn civilize, separating us from the beasts (253). Aristotle's *On Rhetoric* still tells us how to arrive at the best possible means of persuasion in any given case, and although Aristotle never quite says that good rhetoric may be defined only by whether it prevails, his point is that language is both the tool of the powerful and the means to power.

Literacy research over the last few decades indicates that reading and writing cannot exist apart from ideology and politics, from, in other words, questions of power: Who decides what books citizens or parishioners or students will read and which interpretations will be deemed legitimate; who decides what can be written, in what dialect, in what form, by whom; who decides which students or which citizens may have access to which literacies, if any at all; which literacies are valorized and which ones ignored or disparaged. There is no neutral literacy. Literacy is always already embedded in particular social structures, instantiating the values of particular groups and cultures, which are themselves organized in response to power.

Spirituality—as distinct from religion, ethics, or morality—seems to derive from the recognition of human power*lessness* in the face of nature or other realities of human life and is concerned with attaining the kind of personal power that allows individuals to survive the vicissitudes of this life and to attain inner peace. In *The Clerk's Tale*, Chaucer calls it "pacience in adversitee"; in the *Boece*, he explains it this way:

> Thanne yif hit so be that thow art myhty over thiself (*that is to seyn, by tranquillite of thy sowle*), than hast thow thinge in thi power that thow noldest never leesen, ne Fortune ne may nat beneme it the. (2.4, 136–40)

It was, in fact, work on *The Clerk's Tale* that helped me see that spirituality is not some transhistorical nirvana separated from such concerns as culture, gender, class, and race. In an ideal society, the struggle to achieve "tranquillite"—what Al-Anon calls serenity— and at the same time to live *in* the world would be equally arduous for all of us. But the problems that beset human beings are bound up in the material conditions under which they live. In the real world, men's and women's experiences—their realities—are different, and thus their spiritual struggles are different. For Chaucer's Griselda as for most women, there is little if any escape into some ascetic retreat. Not only do women contend with their own biology but also in patriarchal societies, where sex roles are strictly defined and prescribed, women wrestle as well with externally imposed expectations and limitations different from those men face. In recent years, some theologians, aware of the cultural conditioning of women, have discussed "the refusal to love oneself well, the refusal to celebrate both one's dignity and one's responsibility" as a distinctly female sin (Fox 120). While my interest in spirituality takes a decidedly feminist cast, this issue could, I think, just as easily be approached from the perspective of class, race, ethnicity, sexual orientation, or region. While it may well be that the deepest spiritual experiences occur in some realm before or beyond language, it is also true that communicating these experiences depends on language, words that, while perhaps inadequate, are never neutral but always sermonic, ideological, rhetorical, and thus always related, though often covertly, to issues of power.

In the late eighties, these strands—my academic interests and my private concerns—came together. Shirley Brice Heath's work had shown that there is much to learn—much academic theorists had not considered—in investigating the language and literacy of "ordinary" people. Radway had demonstrated that studying the reading practices of actual women could tell us about the complex and contradictory uses and functions of reading in women's lives. With this background, I began to realize that I knew women who used their literacy in ways the research neglected—women who wrote and read for spiritual purposes. Suddenly, interesting questions emerged from the overlay of rhetoric, literacy, spirituality, and gender, most of them having to do with meaning and power. I decided to ask some of the Mountain City Al-Anon women to tell me how they used their literacy in their spiritual lives and what they thought about their reading and writing. Listening to their stories, I was reminded, and still am, of the opening paragraph of *Diving Deep and Surfacing,* by theologian Carol Christ:

> Women's stories have not been told. And without stories there is no articulation of experience. . . . Without stories [a woman] cannot understand herself. Without stories she is alienated from those deeper experiences of self and world that have been called spiritual or religious. She is closed in silence. . . . If women's stories are not told, the depths of women's souls will not be known. (1)

The purpose of this book, this little narrative, is to tell the stories of these Al-Anon women who use literacy in reshaping their lives.

Telling the Stories

As a little narrative, this book focuses on specific literate practices engaged in by six actual women in a particular time and place. Let me describe the time and place.

When I lived in Mountain City in the late eighties, the nearby coal mines were downsizing as the operators increased technology to replace union workers. Glass factories in the region had closed; the building that had housed one in Mountain City was being turned into a shopping mall. The general area was losing population. According to the 1980 U.S. census, Mountain City had a population of 27,605, and the county had 75,024 persons. In 1990, the population of Mountain City was 25,879, a decline of six percent; the county numbered 75,509, a slight increase. The university generally adds an extra 18,000 to 19,000 students to the population during the academic year and is also, along with the university medical center, the area's major employer.

Though the university brings some economic stability to the immediate vicinity, Mountain City lagged behind the rest of the nation economically. The surrounding rural areas and small towns suffered from the traditional problems of the region's poverty. In 1979, the median household income in Mountain City was $16,296; for the U.S. overall, the figure was $17,710 in 1980. In 1989, median household income had risen to $18,022 in Mountain City but to $30,056 nationally in 1990. In 1979 the per capita income of Mountain City was $6,015, compared to the national per capita figure in 1980 of $7,787; in 1989 Mountain City's per capita income was $10,533, almost $4000 less than the U.S. per capita income of $14,420 in 1990.

Although the area was home to visible minorities of people of Italian and Eastern European descent whose forbears had come for jobs in the mines, the racial composition lacked variation. In 1980 the city itself was ninety-four percent white, while the county was ninety-six percent white. In 1990, the city was ninety-two percent white, and the county ninety-five percent white. As one might expect, because of the university, the educational level of the city itself was higher than that of the surrounding areas. In 1980, seventy-eight percent of the city population over age twenty-five had completed high school, and sixty-six percent of the county population had done so. In 1990, eighty-five percent of the city population over age twenty-five had completed high school, while seventy-five percent of the county population had.

The women who talked to me are, I would say, typical of this profile, as I explain in more detail in chapter 1. Four of the women —Jennifer, Jill, Judy, and Tommie—were natives of the region, though none of them had grown up in Mountain City. Lilly and Catherine were outsiders—from the Midwest and the East Coast, respectively—who had come to Mountain City because of their husbands' faculty positions at the university. Catherine, Jennifer, and Lilly held undergraduate degrees; Jill was enrolled, majoring in social work. Jennifer was in graduate school. Judy had finished high school and had taken a cosmetology course. Tommie had passed her GED. In the next chapter, I talk a bit more about the economic situation of each of the women.

Chapter 1, "A Dais for My Words," explains how I carried out my research; appendix B, "An Essay on Research and Telling the

Truth," takes up the problems encountered along the way and the ethical dilemmas that had to be resolved in writing about my findings. In chapter 1, I include some detail about my research participants and my relationship with them. Although I do not cite her work extensively, I want to acknowledge here how important to this project was Ann Oakley's writing on women researchers interviewing women research participants. Oakley's work gave me the confidence early on to deviate from male models of research, which demand the researcher adopt an "objective" and "distanced" stance. In appendix B, I elaborate on this issue and related ones—narration and representation, the mismatch between words and referents, the possibility of doing inquiry—by drawing on sociologist Dorothy E. Smith's idea of the social construction of both the object and the subject in her defense of inquiry in the postmodern age.

Chapters 2 and 3 are the "meat" of the research, focusing, respectively, on the writing and then the reading of the Mountain City Al-Anon women. Both chapters demonstrate that in these women's lives, reading and writing and talking are intertwined, embedded in one another in rich and complex ways. Chapter 2, "Composing (as) Power," takes up the issue of personal writing, a topic to which the response from composition studies has been ambivalent. In this chapter, I trace the writing the Mountain City women do in three stages of their spiritual journey—healing, letting go of old resentments and outmoded standards, and developing a language, or voice, by which to "carry the message." In chapter 3, I draw on Louise Rosenblatt's notion of aesthetic and efferent reading and on the work of other reader-response critics to show that the Mountain City women regard "Reading as a Matter of Life." I discuss the roles of reading and talking about reading in the creation of a mutually empowering community among the Mountain City women.

Chapter 4, "Power as Positive and Available," looks at the social nature of the Mountain City women's literacy. Beginning with Sylvia Scribner's notion of three metaphors of literacy, I argue that for my research participants, "literacy as state of grace" leads to both "literacy as adaptation" and "literacy as power." I draw on Cornel West in explaining what power means in this context. In the final chapter,

"Literacy Lessons," the discussion turns to the implications of my project for theory, research, and pedagogy. I comment on the transformative quality of literacy, using Wlad Godzich's notion that literacy is "subject-constituting" but modifying it with Smith's view of the subject as less individuated and more social than Godzich's.

The little narratives of literacy, including the one I offer here, show "how individuals and groups engage in self-formation not as an autonomous activity but as a practice of everyday life" (Trimbur 130–31). My aim is in the next chapters is to allow the Mountain City women to describe the literate practices they use in their spiritual lives so that as writing teachers we may have a more thorough knowledge of the uses and functions of reading and writing in our culture.

1 / A Dais for My Words

In 1986 shortly after finishing my dissertation—which was a theoretical and political analysis of Walter Ong's "great leap" theory of literacy—I moved from Austin to the city I now refer to as Mountain City. As in Austin, in Mountain City I attended Al-Anon meetings. Because Al-Anon claims to be a spiritual program, much of the talk that goes on in these meetings has to do with participants' individual and shared perceptions of God, or, in their words, "my higher power." What became obvious in the Mountain City Al-Anon meetings that I had not noticed in the Austin meetings—not because it wasn't there but because of the myopia that seems to infect all dissertation writers—was that there was, as well, much talk about literacy: The women—and in Mountain City it was almost all women—who attended Al-Anon meetings kept telling each other to "read the literature"; they talked about writing not only "the searching and fearless moral inventory" required by the Fourth Step but also journals, letters to make amends, and prayers.

After two years, I moved away. About this same time, I heard Ann Berthoff explain at the Conference on College Composition and Communication that Paulo Freire's pedagogy of the oppressed comes not just from his Marxism but from his Catholicism as well. In that moment, I realized why Freire's concept of literacy is so powerful: It taps into that striving in his students, in his teachers, and in his readers for something beyond themselves, which is a pretty fair definition of spirituality. A few months after leaving Mountain City, I used the link between spirituality and literacy to read James Moffett's *Storm in the Mountains: A Case Study of Censorship, Conflict, and Consciousness,* a book that shows that when schools don't take into account the religious beliefs of the people they serve, the effect on literacy learning can be profound ("Literacy").

Shortly after I moved to South Carolina, a local adult-literacy volunteer told me that he had attended every country church in Oconee County; the first thing his adult students wanted to do with their newly acquired skills, he said, was to read Scripture in church, and they always invited him.

Because the research into contemporary literacy in the mid-to-late 1980s seemed to treat religion and spirituality as only a peripheral issue, these connections between literacy and spirituality were intriguing. I decided to investigate. During three summers, with research grants from Clemson University and from its English Department, I traveled back to Mountain City to interview some of the Al-Anon women I knew there about how they use reading and writing in their spiritual lives.

The research I planned yielded so much more information than I had imagined that transcribing the data and doing an initial analysis took far longer than I had thought it would. I realized early on that the research data could support a book-length manuscript rather than the one or two articles I had originally envisioned but that I would need more sophisticated analytical tools than I possessed at that time. Consequently, I have spent a lot of time over the last decade reading.

This chapter explains how I carried out my research. I include some detail about my research participants and about my relationship with them. Discussion of problems I encountered and of some of the ethical dilemmas that confronted me appears in appendix B, "An Essay on Research and Telling the Truth." There I take up methodological problems, such as the nature of case study research, and the philosophical difficulty of the relationship of inquiry and truth.

The Research

The data for this book come from two separate interviews with five research participants and one interview with an additional person. The interviews with the first five women, whose pseudonyms are Catherine, Jennifer, Jill, Judy, and Tommie, took place in the summers of 1990 and 1991; the interview with the final participant, whom I call Lilly, occurred in 1992. Catherine, Judy, and Tommie talked with me in their homes; the interviews with Jennifer, Jill, and Lilly took place in the houses where I stayed while I was in Mountain City. To guide the interviews, I used previously prepared lists of questions; these questions were handwritten on a yellow legal pad under rubrics such as reading, writing, spiritual/spirituality, stories, language, education, feminism, power, and family. Because of the informal nature of these interviews, however, the questions were rarely asked in the order I had planned or in the same order from one research participant to the next. The order of the questions I asked or of the topics I introduced surely must influence the responses, though I can not venture to say how. Although I did not follow any strict order, I did elicit responses to all the questions from all the women.

I taped the interviews using a portable cassette recorder. The tapes are full of starts and stops, ice tinkling in tea glasses, phones ringing, dogs barking, children yelling. In *The Tape-Recorded Interview*, Edward Ives advises not to try to save tape by turning off the recorder during interruptions (59). I did turn it off, however, when the women received phone calls from family members, businesses, or people they sponsored in Al-Anon: these conversations seemed to me at the time either irrelevant or private, in either case not something I would or could legitimately include in my tapes. Because I inadvertently erased one side of the tape of the interview with Lilly (thereby causing myself a near heart attack), a replacement interview was done the next day as she drove me to the airport two hours away.

During the interviews, I took notes in addition to the taping. Immediately after each interview, I used those largely illegible scribblings to make another set of fairly detailed (and somewhat more legible) notes. This served as the basis for what Ives calls a catalog, that is, a "detailed summary of what is on the tape—a complete précis" (90), the purpose of which is to help the researcher or others locate material on an audiotape (92). After returning to Clemson, I listened to the tapes many times and made the catalogs of each interview more complete. The first versions are handwritten. Then I transferred the catalogs to floppy disks. After adding still more detail to these catalogs, I used those notes to transcribe the parts of the interviews I believed to be relevant.

Because with these five participants virtually no inconsistencies occurred between the 1990 and the 1991 interviews, I decided not to transcribe any of the second set of interviews. In addition, long reminiscences about childhood, digressions about parents' health, stories about children's achievements, conversations about current events, food, or mutual friends, as well as inquiries and responses about my life, were not included in the transcripts. Because these women were acquaintances and friends I had seen once or twice a week for the two years I had lived in Mountain City, the interviews were actually embedded in the sorts of conversations friends have when they haven't seen each other for a while; the purely social exchanges did not become part of the transcripts. Certainly these topics have some bearing on the identities of these women and on their comments about their literate and spiritual practice. Yet, in the years I've worked with this material, I have not found it necessary or helpful to include information from those conversations. Though I aimed at accuracy, *uhs*, *ers*, *you knows*, pauses, sighs, and laughs, like the extraneous conversations, were left out. In the transcripts, I often edited my questions down to the essential point. Again, all of these omissions influence the data and the conclusions I draw. I use only the transcripts as I write about this research, only occasionally going back to the original tapes for clarification.

In accordance with accepted research practice and the rules of Clemson University's Committee for the Protection of Human Subjects, I explained at the beginning of each interview the purpose of my work and promised anonymity, trying to make it clear that I would use the women's words in presentations and publications. I tried very hard to give the Mountain City women an out, to let each know that if at any point she became uncomfortable, she could withdraw temporarily or permanently. In fact, each was required to read and sign a statement to this effect, which I have filed with the Human Subjects Committee at Clemson. Once the women realized

I would be talking or writing about their experiences to academic audiences, each one, without exception, responded with some variation of: "Well, Beth, I just can't imagine that anything I would say could possibly help you with your work. But, if other people are going to read it or hear it, then what I say might help somebody else. So, sure." They see the interviews and my subsequent work with that material as the "carry[ing] this message to others" part of the Twelfth Step. In fact, once, in 1995, when I was writing about this issue and consulted the Mountain City women, Tommie said in a phone conversation, "Your doing this work gives me a dais for my words."

Anonymity

Nonetheless, my first concern in asking Al-Anon members to serve as research participants in my project was anonymity. Al-Anon's Eleventh Tradition reads: "Our public relations policy is based on attraction rather than promotion; we need always maintain personal anonymity at the level of press, radio, TV, and film. We need guard with special care the anonymity of all AA members." Because of this tradition, I worried about this project from the beginning, from even before the beginning, finding encouragement, finally, to go forward in Nan Robertson's explanation of how she resolved a similar situation.

In *Getting Better: Inside Alcoholics Anonymous*, Robertson, an AA member, tells of explaining to Lois Wilson, widow of AA founder Bill Wilson, her decision to write about AA. Lois, as she was known in AA and Al-Anon circles, was concerned, reminding Robertson that "the eleventh tradition warns against breaking even one's own anonymity at the public level, in print or broadcasts" (18). Robertson promised to protect every AA member she wrote about but told Lois, "I think the disclosure of my own affiliation should be a matter between me and my own conscience" (18). AA and Al-Anon members who treat these organizations as secret may not, therefore, approve of my work, but my Mountain City friends are comfortable with my telling their stories as long as mine is the only anonymity I break. This is the reason I did not ask for samples of the Mountain City women's private writing; Fourth Steps, journals, letters, and God Can notes are too private to be published, revealing, as they would, both intimate and public details by which the women could be identified.

Once I began the project, the idea of *not* disseminating what I was learning about these extracurricular uses of reading and writing never really seemed an option for me. We don't know nearly enough about what it means to be or become literate in American culture, and in academic discussions, contemporary spiritual uses of literacy have often received short shrift. This "little narrative" of literacy— about particular persons reading and writing in one specific place and in one time for one purpose—may combine with other little narratives of literacy to give a richer, more nuanced picture of how reading and writing work in the lives of actual rather than theoretical human beings. Pulled to tell the story and at the same time to protect my research participants' anonymity, I am careful, as I write up this research, to use pseudonyms, to change some details, and to omit certain others.

As I have written papers and chapters of this book, I have called and/or sent copies to my research participants asking for correction or clarification. Tommie complained that my "Composing (as) Power" conference paper had not included enough in one place where I quoted her. I omitted the offending statement from the published version because I didn't have the space to include what Tommie thought I needed in order to represent her ideas accurately. Lilly voiced her disappointment that I had omitted in the published version of that paper what she called the "messy middles." I have certainly included more detail in the greatly expanded version I present in chapter 2. I hope that it is enough to satisfy Tommie and Lilly, both having taught me much about the value of complexity, ambiguity, and process. If they disapprove, though, they have not said so. In appendix B, I take up the ethical issue that concerns me most in writing about this research: the tension between imposing order on the data and representing as honestly as I can these women's perceptions of their experiences.

For me, one important question about this project has been this: Am I presuming on friendships? Yes, I am. I could not have done this research if these women had not known me. The Mountain City Al-Anon women talked to me in a way I don't think they would talk to a stranger. Yes, I have benefited from the research. Have they? They tell me they have. Two or three have said that they had not realized the importance of words, of reading, and of writing until I began to ask about theirs. Jill, for example, says she values her writing much more now than she did before. According to Lilly, I serve as a mirror for the "communion of friendship" these women share: My view of them as a community created to a large degree through their literate practices has given them a new way to see themselves and their relationships with one another.

But other issues are significant. Some readers might question whether I did the research at Al-Anon meetings. Despite my unabashed belief, on the one hand, that everything should be examined, I have qualms about using AA and Al-Anon meetings as research sites. Indeed when the issue of allowing researchers to observe meetings has come up, as it inevitably does in meetings in university towns, I have sometimes voted to exclude them—not to deprive them of a chance to study these groups but to preserve the requisite privacy and anonymity for the free exchange of ideas within the group. In addition, as an Al-Anon insider, I might also argue that two or three visits to a Twelve-Step meeting will provide neither accuracy nor understanding.

That I have attended Al-Anon meetings serves as background, certainly, and gave me access to my research participants. I first met all of the women who talked with me for this project at meetings. Before this research project began, several of the women who later became my research participants approached me with their writing. Once when I gave her a ride home from a meeting, Tommie invited me in to listen to some poems she had written. Judy asked me to edit an essay she was writing for an Al-Anon publication. Jill requested my help with a piece she had written for a brochure on childhood sexual abuse. One academic friend has suggested that these women sought me out because my status as English professor could certify their literacy. The others—Jennifer, Catherine, and Lilly—were people I approached because I knew from my acquaintance with each of them that reading and writing were important parts of their practice of the Al-Anon program. Jennifer used to call me up to talk about what words mean: "How would you define reconciliation? What do you think the difference is between stubbornness and perseverance?" Once or twice, Catherine shared long entries in her journal. Lilly talked a great deal about books and plays.

I want to be very clear: I did not do my research at Al-Anon meetings.

Ideology

In addition to anonymity, two other issues, both ideological, were important for me and may well be for readers, too. The first is gender. Some critics of Al-Anon question its use of masculine pronouns for God. This is a problem for feminists in many traditions, and I know of no satisfactory solution. One Episcopal friend sings each Sunday morning, "Blessed is *she* who comes in the name of the Lord," while I myself change the pronouns in the Nicene Creed referring to the Holy Spirit. Neither modification solves the problem, but with these strategies, we each claim some small space in a religion that seems almost unrelentingly male and exclusionary. An Al-Anon meeting I regularly attended in Austin during the mid-eighties tried to solve the problem by using "He/She/It" to refer to God, but this usage apparently hasn't caught on widely. Subscribing to any tradition includes coming to terms with complex issues of language, gender, and power. Like people in other organizations, women and men in Twelve-Step programs continue to grapple with these linguistic issues in various ways.

A related issue is Al-Anon's Fourth Step, "Made a searching and fearless moral inventory of ourselves," which feminists often see as a negative for women. Indeed, according to Edmund B. O'Reilly's account of AA testimonies, some women and people of color say that "their drink and recovery experiences are not congruent with models and assumptions in AA policy" (11). These AA members argue that the need for humility, regarded as necessary for sobriety for the (white?) men in AA and achieved by working the Fourth Step, should be matched by the need for *women in AA* to understand not just their weaknesses but also their strengths (O'Reilly 12, my emphasis). In fact, most *Al-Anon* discussions of the Fourth Step emphasize listing assets as well as liabilities. The distinction between the two programs is important in regard to this issue: The women I talked with were not AA members. Sometimes, critics are not aware of the differences between the two programs.

Similarly, a *CCC* Anonymous critic, an AA member herself, complains that the thesis of my "Composing (as) Power" article— that is, by using writing in their spiritual lives, my research participants attain a kind of power—is "somewhat ironic, since both in Al-Anon and AA admitting 'powerlessness' is the first step to recovery" (282). *Paradoxical* is a better word, I think, than ironic. Some feminists critics argue that admitting powerlessness is dangerous for women in Al-Anon because the alcoholic in their lives is often a husband, sometimes an abusive one. People who say this invariably neglect the Eleventh Step. In the First Step—"We admitted we were *powerless* over alcohol—that our lives had become unmanageable" (my emphasis)—people admit their personal powerlessness over alcoholism, their own or somebody else's; in the Eleventh Step— "Sought through prayer and meditation to improve our conscious contact with God *as we understood Him,* praying only for knowledge of His will for us and the *power* to carry that out" (again, my emphasis on the word *power*)—they are assured of access to a spiritual power that allows them to proceed with their lives with choice and dignity. Paradoxical language like this bothers some people, but every spiritual tradition I am familiar with speaks in paradoxes, which, apparently, one has to experience before one understands; as a recent commentary puts it, "Paradox is the nature of spiritual life" (Kurtz and Ketcham 18).

In addition, understanding the notion of powerlessness from an Al-Anon perspective requires taking into account the interdependence of literacy and orality in the program, where written materials without the oral teachings can be almost misleading. (George A.

Jensen makes a similar point about the written materials of AA.)
In Al-Anon meetings I have attended across the country, a distinction is made between powerlessness and helplessness: While a person may be powerless over other human beings, as oldtimers explain, she is never helpless. The Mountain City Al-Anon women
talk a great deal about choices—discovering them, making them,
taking responsibility for them. At one point in the interview, Tommie
says, describing herself previous to joining Al-Anon, "I didn't know
I had a choice." Picking up the William Coles language I quote
at the end of the "Composing" article (and use again at the end
of chapter 2), Lilly wrote, on being told of Anonymous's objections, "She doesn't seem to feel that we can ' . . . have the power to
choose with awareness, to change and adapt consciously, and in this
sense to be able to have a share in determining [our] own destiny'"
(Coles 253).

Al-Anon oral teachings focus not just on the first line of the
Serenity Prayer, "the serenity to accept the things I cannot change,"
but also on its second line, "the courage to change the things I can."
In Al-Anon meetings, there is much talk of differentiating between
those things that cannot be changed and those that can and about
specific ways to make those changes. Seeing published statements
without the context of the oral teachings, casual visitors or outside
examiners can easily fall into the error of denying agency to Al-
Anon members. In fact, failing to recognize the agency of others
seems to be an especial temptation for academics who write about
people different from ourselves.

In addition, the sexism in AA and Al-Anon literature is a concern for some—including many Al-Anon members. In a *Signs* article
on the ideology of Al-Anon, Janice Haarken explains that the earliest Al-Anon literature was written in the 1950s from a prefeminist
perspective. During the 1970s, Al-Anon was influenced by feminist critiques, Haarken points out. The result is a double message:
Even as the first Al-Anon daily reader, *One Day at a Time in Al-
Anon* (ODAT), copyrighted in 1973, exhorts members to see themselves as "responsible only to [a] 'higher power'" (Haarken 335), it
nonetheless continues to encourage wives of alcoholics to play the

traditional self-sacrificing, "wifely" role and keep the family together. In chapter 3, Lilly reports that such advice once made her so angry that she threw the book across the room. Clearly, many in Al-Anon are not heeding the old advice, for in meetings across the country, I am told, when informal polls are taken of who stayed with an alcoholic spouse and who left, the results are about half and half, somewhat higher than the divorce rate in the general population. According to my research participants, no one is ever advised to stay if there is physical abuse.

Haarken's critique argues that the politics of Al-Anon and similar groups is contradictory: It is feminist in that these groups

> attract primarily women, draw implicitly on a critique of patriarchy, stress the importance of egalitarian relationships with men, provide support for women's emancipatory struggles against personal domination, and offer a challenge to traditional institutions and the family. (324)

At the same time, the politics of these groups is conservative in that these programs

> signif[y] the containment of [feminist] impulses within an ideology that preserves nostalgic conceptions of the family as the vehicle for personal redemption. (329)

In addition, Haarken carefully distinguishes between the literature of the Twelve-Step groups, "where relationships of mutual support are formed," and "the mass marketing of these ideas" by self-proclaimed self-help authors (340), who more often than not stress "the pathology of the caregiver" (341). Many critics do not make that distinction, lumping together all self-help materials.

The language of *Alcoholics Anonymous* (aka the Big Book, first published in 1939), is, I said in my *CCC* Response to Anonymous, so obviously sexist and condescending in regard to women—in a black-and-white-1930s-movie sort of way—that I am less angered or upset by it than amused: All the early AAers were apparently

married to "wonderful girls" or "swell gals," who struggled heroi-
cally to pay the bills and raise the children alone, until their irresponsible husbands found recovery in AA. The AA Big Book, like
any other written text, is a product of its times, instantiating both
conscious and unconscious desires and attitudes not only of the
writer but also of the culture. Do we throw out the spiritual insights
of Bill Wilson because his language was sexist and his attitude toward his wife and other women was, by our current standards, ret-
rograde? Certainly oppressive messages exist in AA and Al-Anon,
but the point I want to make is that my research participants sub-
vert those messages. In a complicated literacy act, they have, as I
argued in the *CCC* Response, stolen Prospero's books.

The ideological issue in regard to AA and Al-Anon that is, in
my experience, harder to deal with than gender is class. In *Getting
Better,* Robertson traces the background of AA's founders, Bill Wilson and Bob Smith: "They were Anglo-Saxon Protestants, middle-
class to the core, and political and economic conservatives" (35).
While neither came from particularly privileged backgrounds, both
were educated beyond the average for their times. Because of their
drinking and the Depression, both had serious financial problems,
though their work would ordinarily have brought monetary reward:
Wilson worked on Wall Street, and Smith was a physician. In the
early years, AA's membership mirrored the background of these
two men. In the forties and fifties—and especially in more recent
decades—however, as word spread of AA's success, members were
attracted from all regions of America and began to reflect the country's diversity. This means not just racial, religious, regional, or ethnic variation. It also means social class.

Yet, in AA and subsequently in Al-Anon, the official ideology is
that class doesn't exist. As Robertson explains,

> In the subculture that is AA, most of the world's yardsticks
> for success do not count. Members usually do not ask oth-
> ers about their age, occupation or profession, where they
> work or where they went to school. The clothes a person
> wears, the way he handles language, the size of his bank

account, the honors he may have won are not important in
AA. Additionally, there is a kind of "keeping down with the
Joneses" attitude. (124)

The women I interviewed rigorously subscribed to this attitude.
The few questions I asked that touched overtly on class were re-
buffed by the research participants. This attitude was stated most
assertively by Lilly, the sixties' activist, who, interestingly, has more
money and social prestige than the other women I interviewed. The
Mountain City women were at the same time scrupulously honest
about their own economic situations: Both Tommie and Jennifer say
that they cannot afford subscriptions to magazines and newspapers.
Aware of her own status, Lilly says that her college philosophy of
Whoever Has, Pays can only work up to certain point: "I can be too
generous, and that can hurt me and anybody I'm giving to. I've
learned a lot about giving too much." She continues, however: "But
books are really different. If I have a book that somebody doesn't
have, they can always borrow it."

In Al-Anon testimonies and in discussions in meetings, members sometimes talk about class consciousness but only as one of
"the defects of character" that Step Six says one should become entirely ready to have God remove. In large cities, meetings reflect the
ethnicity and socioeconomic status of the surrounding neighborhood. In a town the size of Mountain City, meetings draw from
across class boundaries that often separate people in other parts of
their lives. Indications of these boundaries are aggressively ignored.
Robertson explains the reason for this phenomenon in her sketch of
the similarities between Wilson and Smith: "[T]heir special bond
was one of identical suffering. . . . Men in war—indeed anyone who
had lived through a particularly intense and frightening experience
—can understand this bond of memory and gratitude. It is perpetu-
ated endlessly in AA" (35). This is true also among the Mountain
City Al-Anon women—across lines of income, education, profes-
sion, houses, clothes, neighborhoods, and other social and cultural
indices of success.

To elicit the kind of information needed to write about class

among these women, I would have risked their trust and consequently the information about literacy and spirituality they did so
generously offer. So it is that my study of this group of Al-Anon
women neglects in important ways issues of class. To be sure, such
a study would be valuable, but it is not my project.

The Women

I met half the women who became my research participants within
the first couple of weeks of my move in 1986 to Mountain City. Immediately after arriving, I attended a nearby Al-Anon conference
where I clearly remember meeting Tommie and Catherine. Tommie
led a workshop session that I attended, and I remember thinking
that her calm manner, her deep insight into family dynamics, her
openness about her own experience, and her articulate presentation
indicated that she was probably a therapist. Tommie has a GED. My
first impression reveals a great deal about my own biases and values,
not to say snobberies. (In fact, as readers will discover, the ability to
speak clearly and openly is a trait that all my research participants
share. In the interviews, Jill expresses concern that newcomers to
Al-Anon might be put off by the level of language in the meetings:
"We are all so eloquent," she remarks.)

In 1990, when I interviewed Tommie, she was forty-one years
old and had been in Al-Anon for six years. She was married to her
second husband, who, still drinking, was working then as a taxi
driver. Tommie has three children: at the time of the interviews, a
married daughter in her twenties from Tommie's first marriage and
two teenaged sons from the second. Tommie speaks with no embar-
rassment of a childhood of poverty, including welfare and housing
projects. Tommie had worked many kinds of jobs in her life, mainly
waiting tables, but at the time of the interviews, she was not working outside her home. By sociological standards, Tommie and her
family would be classified as part of "the working poor."

Catherine, in 1990, was fifty-three years old, separated from her
scientist husband, whose long-term alcoholism had been interrupted
by his dean's order to enter treatment. At the time of the interviews,

his sobriety was, I gathered, still fragile. Catherine saw her husband as a real intellectual and herself as his inferior, even though they both held undergraduate degrees from the same prestigious college. Catherine and her husband have three daughters, two who were already professionals and one who was an undergraduate at an Ivy League university. Despite her husband's professional achievements, Catherine lived simply in the small house they had shared since their move to Mountain City. Catherine had taught elementary school after her marriage while her husband was in graduate school. After she began having children, she considered herself a full-time mother, except for stints of volunteer work, including, interestingly, work as a literacy volunteer. During the time of the interviews, Catherine was working part-time in a bookstore. Catherine, as we see in the following chapters, is a devout Catholic.

Jennifer was another acquaintance from very early in my Mountain City experience. Although I now have no clear memory of the first time I met Jen, I do remember that she helped me find the dry cleaners, the haircutter, and the dentist. I have a vivid memory of her helping me shop for a coat warm enough for the local winters. When I met Jen in 1986, she was a secretary on campus, married to a man in AA who was working as a drug and alcohol counselor in a nearby hospital. Jen had a BA from the university. She had grown up two hours away in the state capital. In 1990, she was thirty-seven years old, childless, and divorced, about halfway through a masters degree in counseling. She had been in Al-Anon for almost seven years. At the time of the interviews, Jennifer was living on a small, temporary alimony payment in an apartment in a student neighborhood.

I'd heard of Lilly before I actually met her. Al-Anon members in Mountain City talked about her a great deal, both in meetings and in private conversations ("Remember the story Lilly tells about . . . "; "Lilly always says . . . "). Actually, they invoked Lilly even more than I realized, because for many of them she was their sponsor —that is, combination confidant, guide to the Al-Anon program, counselor, and spiritual advisor—and often in speech they referred to her as "my sponsor" rather than by name. Several weeks after I arrived in Mountain City, I finally managed to put the name with a face, saying to myself, "So this woman is the one they've all been talking about." For a semester during my time in Mountain City, because of the flexibility of my teaching schedule, I drove with Lilly to a morning Al-Anon meeting in a nearby town. Lilly liked this meeting because it attracted a number of oldtimers; in Mountain City, Lilly was the oldtimer. From the conversations on these trips, I began to see Lilly's influence on the reading of several of the other Al-Anon women I knew. Lilly has a degree from a Catholic woman's college in the Midwest.

Lilly was married to a successful law professor, a man whose work is widely known in his field but whose career had nearly been lost because of his addictions. The two had met in the late sixties in New York when he was in law school and Lilly was working in theater and for various leftist causes. They had lived together for more than a decade before marrying. In 1992, they had been married ten years and had two small children. When I interviewed her, Lilly was forty-six years old and had been in the program for nine years. During the time I knew her in Mountain City and during the years of the interviews, Lilly described her work as "talking to people" during the hours that her children were in school. By this, she meant serving as Al-Anon sponsor to a large number of women. As I paid attention to the transcripts of the interviews, I came to see Lilly as a volunteer informal counselor-therapist-priest-friend to many women who showed up at Al-Anon searching for a better way to live.

As with Lilly, my acquaintance with Judy didn't occur right away, though people in meetings mentioned her often because she had more years in Mountain City Al-Anon than anyone else. Like Lilly, Judy didn't attend many night meetings because of family responsibilities. In 1990, she was forty years old, married, with one child, a teenaged daughter. At the time of the first round of interviews, Judy, a high school graduate who had studied and practiced cosmetology before her marriage, had recently resigned a managerial position with a local supermarket because of an upcoming move to another town. Involved in the program for nine years, Judy and her husband, who worked for the gas company, were a well-known couple in Al-Anon and AA circles in and around Mountain City; both were active in what is called service work, that is, holding administrative offices, and both regularly spoke at meetings around the area. Judy had been diagnosed with diabetes during her pregnancy and as a result of this chronic condition has suffered a number of health problems.

I didn't meet Jill until my second year in Mountain City, and so at the time of the interviews knew her less well than I knew the others. My first clear memory of Jill is of her approaching me after a meeting and telling me that her sponsor had suggested that she ask me to look at something she was writing for a therapy group for women who had been sexually abused. I did so and found her writing powerful, clear, and understated. At the time of the 1990 interview, Jill was about to turn thirty-five and had been in Al-Anon for three years. She was married to her second husband, who had been sober in AA about six months. Jill had three children. The older two, from her first marriage, were teenagers, and her youngest was eight. During a recent separation from her husband, Jill had started back to school and was taking a variety of courses, in both general education and social work.

The Mountain City women who talked with me knew a great deal about my life; they knew my values and beliefs, my experiences, and my own language use in a variety of settings. I believe that for them my first and chief identity was another Al-Anon member. The interviews, as I stated earlier, were more like conversations between old friends than formal sessions conducted by a social scientist; preparing for the interviews, I had taken to heart Ann Oakley's advice:

> [W]hen a feminist interviews women, . . . it becomes clear that, in most cases, the goal of finding out about people through interviewing is best achieved when the relationship of interviewer and interviewee is non-hierarchical and

when the interviewer is prepared to invest his or her own
personal identity in the relationship. (41)

My research participants and I had already invested in the relationship.

My aim in *A Communion of Friendship* is to tell the Mountain City
women's stories not as an example of one of the grand narratives of
literacy, where they necessarily become smarter or freer, but rather
as a little narrative, where a particular group of women use their
literacy in specific ways as part of a program they have voluntarily
chosen as a way a make their lives better. In the following chapters,
I share what I found and do some theorizing about what I found.

Seeing how and why writing and reading are used by people
outside the academy will, I hope, enrich our sense of what literacy
is and can be in our culture. As I show in the next chapters, the
women I interviewed use texts, their own and other people's, "to
make sense of their lives" (Brodkey, "Writing" 47), to engage in self-
formation (Trimbur 130), to become agents in their own lives, to
establish community. In the next chapters, I am guided by the notion that all of us need familiarity with—to borrow Clifford Geertz's
language—"the imaginative universe within which [other people's]
acts are signs" (13).

2 / Composing (as) Power

According to historical studies by Jack Goody, Harvey Graff, and Daniel Resnick and Lauren Resnick, spiritual and religious motives have traditionally impelled human beings to seek literacy and, in America, to enact statutes that require it. All over the United States, adult-literacy workers testify to their students' religious motives for learning to read. In addition to such clearly religious connections, a relationship between literacy and spirituality—spirituality defined here as a nonsectarian search for something higher than one's everyday concerns—shows up in trade books like Christina Baldwin's *Life's Companion: Journal Writing as a Spiritual Quest*. Self-help books often call for writing as a part of healing spiritually, though it is not always clear what the term *spiritual* means in these contexts. *Journaling*, as it is called in the self-help and therapeutic literature as well as within some church-sponsored groups, has become an almost commonplace term and practice.

In the last two decades, academic studies have begun to take seriously contemporary interactions of religion or spirituality with literacy. These include Shirley Brice Heath's "Protean Shapes in Literacy Events: Ever-Shifting Oral and Literate Traditions" and *Ways with Words: Language, Life, and Work in Communities and Classrooms*, James Moffett's *Storm in the Mountains: A Case Study of Censorship, Conflict, and Consciousness*, Andrea Fishman's *Amish Literacy: What and How It Means*, Beverly Moss's "Creating a Community: Literacy Events in African-American Churches," and Cushla Kapitzke's *Literacy and Religion: The Textual Politics and Practice of Seventh-Day Adventism*. In the early nineties, there were scattered conference presentations, such as Keith Walters's 1990 paper "Not-So-Hidden Literacy in an Unprogrammed Quaker Meeting" and the 1992 CCCC panel on "Spiritual Sites of Composing," later published in *College Composition and Communication* (Berthoff, Daniell, Campbell, Swearingen, and Moffett). More recently, edited volumes have appeared, like Regina Paxton Foehr and Susan A. Schiller's *The Spiritual Side of Writing: Releasing the Learner's Whole Potential* and Charles M. Anderson and Marian MacCurdy's *Writing and Healing: Toward an Informed Practice.*

Most of these writings did not, however, exist in the late eighties when I first began to think about the gap between, on the one hand, ethnographic studies showing the multiple functions and uses of reading and writing and, on the other, historical studies referencing the links between literacy and religion or spirituality. In order to offer some bridge to that gap, I interviewed the women I knew in Mountain City about how they use literacy in their spiritual lives. Their ages ranged from mid-thirties to mid-fifties. Their education, as I have indicated, went from GED to masters student. They were all practicing members of Al-Anon.

Because reading and writing are significant activities in Al-Anon, because Al-Anon claims that its program is inherently spiritual, and because my research participants had been involved in Al-Anon from three to ten years, I expected them to be able to talk about their spirituality and their reading and writing in the same breath. They did not let me down. I have more than twenty hours of audiotape from the initial interviews (seventeen from the first summer plus three from the interview with Lilly) and an almost equal number from the follow-up conversations.

Analysis of the tapes and of the transcripts made later reveals that spirituality and literacy intertwine in rich and complex ways in these women's lives. For the Mountain City Al-Anon women, there is no such thing as the decontextualized literacy Walter Ong and David Olson describe in their characterization of literacy as something distinct and separate from orality. For the women who were my research participants, reading and writing in Al-Anon are accompanied by and contextualized within orality, not just the talk in meetings but also talk outside meetings with a sponsor or other program friends. In re-forming themselves by means of this Twelve-Step program, my research participants use both written and spoken language—writing and reading, speaking and listening. As they experience what they call *recovery*, they tell stories of their lives to each other and to newcomers. All the Mountain City women who talked to me take seriously the Al-Anon admonition to "share our experience, strength, and hope," and they all articulate a deeply held belief in the power of language to heal and to bring about and deepen spiritual experience. Within the context of all this talk, my research participants read and write. They talk about what they read; they write about what they hear and read; they read about what they hear; they talk about what they write.

They write many different kinds of things. With the qualification that, if pushed too hard, genre lines blur, I have categorized their writings as Fourth Steps, journals, God Can notes, Dear God letters, letters (to be mailed or not), poems, short stories, essays for publication, and school papers. Their written discourses are comprised of one or two words to many thousand. My research participants write or have written all the genres identified above, though, as readers will see, the women do not necessarily share my terminology. They write to come to terms with their emotions, with cultural expectations, and with other people's rules; they write to negotiate their identities; they write to attain group membership; and they write to gain a kind of power, more personal and spiritual than political, but power nonetheless.

I want readers to hear the Mountain City women's voices, but at the same time I want to make the data accessible. At the risk of oversimplifying the rich complexity of the Al-Anon women's perceptions, I have organized this chapter around what seems to be three stages in their spiritual journey. Each stage is perhaps best summarized by a sentence from Tommie: First, "The healing came." Second, "I had to let go of it being perfect, and then it became perfect." And third, "We can't carry our message if we don't have our own language."

"The healing came": Fourth-Step Inventories

The Fourth Step, the "searching and fearless moral inventory," is the most obvious writing assignment in the Al-Anon program and often the first thing that newcomers to Al-Anon write. Many of the

Mountain City women who talked with me found their first sense of healing with this step. The Fourth Step seems to mark the beginning of the end of the personal confusion that brought them to Al-Anon in the first place—for, as Tommie puts it, "You don't come to Al-Anon if you're fine." Of her own Fourth Step, Tommie says:

> I was in such pain. My sponsor said she thought it was extremely important to do a literal, written Fourth Step. She said, "When are you going to forgive yourself? You've got to do a Fourth Step and a Fifth because you are just beating yourself up." But I couldn't write the *Blueprint*.

Blueprint for Progress: Al-Anon's Fourth-Step Inventory, a workbook published by Al-Anon, is designed to help a person look at his or her behaviors and values. Writing out responses to questions in several areas—self-worth, maturity, love, and so forth—is a fairly common way for Al-Anon members to do a Fourth Step. Although this booklet has been helpful to probably thousands of Al-Anon members over the years, the women I talked to seemed more constrained by its particular form than led to self-knowledge by it. Tommie explains her trouble with the *Blueprint:*

> I kept writing the same answers to every question. Then when I focused on the gory details, I got hung up on the completeness of it all. So I had to throw all that away. My first Fourth Step didn't have gory details. I decided: Keep this simple. It didn't have to be everything, it only had to be what I knew. I wrote about a page and a half, an enormous prayer: God, here are the things I don't like about myself. In that Fourth Step was stuff I was afraid to say to anyone. That was the searching moral inventory for me. It worked. The healing came.

Jennie didn't care for the *Blueprint,* either, but unlike Tommie, who invented her own form, Jennie persevered:

The first thing I wrote after getting into the program was connected with my Fourth Step. I used the *Blueprint for Progress*. It was like an English theme. I felt like I was doing an assignment for English class. I could not see any connection between what I was doing and what it was supposed to result in. So to me it wasn't helpful. But it was helpful to my sponsor. My sponsor could make the connections, and she could see what everything was about.

As with many Al-Anon members, Jennie links here the Fourth Step, the inventory, with the Fifth Step, confession ("Admitted to God, to ourselves, and another human being the exact nature of our wrongs"):

I knew it was supposed to be helping me, but I didn't know how or what it was supposed to do. I just gave [my sponsor] the booklet to read. This counted as my Fifth Step. We talked about my answers while she was reading, and we talked about it afterwards.

Even though Jennie sees in retrospect the value of that first Fourth Step, she has found another, more helpful way to write the three or four Fourth Steps she has completed in her seven years in the program: "I do a Fourth Step whenever I get stuck. When something permeates my life, I need to get it on paper so I can determine what the connection is, the similarity. The things that are happening, that I'm having problems with, are usually all the same." The method Jennie uses now and recommends to people she sponsors is the Fourth-Step form in the Big Book of Alcoholics Anonymous. The Big Book form for the Fourth Step includes three columns, the first labeled "I'm resentful at," the second, "The Cause," and the third, "Affects my" (65). Why this form is helpful and Al-Anon's *Blueprint* form is not remains unclear.

While writing seems essential to Jennie's own Fourth Steps, she denies that Fourth Steps have to be written: "I've heard that there are people in town that have never done a written Fourth Step. I

know of one Al-Anon person, most of her Fourth and Fifth Steps
have been verbal. She writes real well. It works for her that way."
Jennifer includes the comment about the writing ability of the
woman she is talking about probably because I had asked earlier in
the interview about people with low literacy skills whom I had observed in meetings in Mountain City. Because Jennie was the first of
the Al-Anon women I interviewed, I did not realize until later that
she was stating themes I would hear again and again: First, though
literacy may expedite growth through the program, it is not necessary; it is the spiritual exercise, not the literacy that brings about the
spiritual awakening promised in the Twelfth Step. And I would
agree: Literacy doesn't automatically bestow anything, neither spiritual insight nor higher forms of cognition. Second, my research
participants insist that there are many ways to do the steps and
work the program, even though one way work may better than another for a particular person at a particular time. There is room, the
Mountain City women say, for individual difference; the abstrac-
tions are guidelines, not hard-and-fast rules.

For Tommie, as for Jennie, part of the healing of the Fourth Step
comes with sharing it with someone in a Fifth Step. "It became part
of sharing and trust," Tommie explains.

> I read this Fourth Step, the enormous prayer, to my spon-
> sor. I was terrified the whole time reading it. I just wanted
> God to forgive me for what I'd done to my kids. I believed
> I was kind and compassionate, and at the same time I be-
> lieved I'd hurt my kids. When I finished, she said, "Is this
> all?" Then she told me she loved me. And that was it.

Since that first Fourth Step, Tommie—perhaps the Al-Anon
person Jennie was talking about?—has discussed her problems and
insights with her sponsor rather writing out a list of "the exact nature of [her] wrongs." Nonetheless, Tommie asks people she now
sponsors "to do at least one literal Fourth Step." She explains why
people have difficulty with this step:

What happens is there's a lot of discussion that seems to center around thoroughness and honesty. It asks for searching, fearless, and moral. It does not ask for complete. That word 'complete' hangs up adult children [of alcoholics]. How complete is complete?

Both Judy and Jill talked at length about the role of the Fourth Step in their spiritual lives, attributing to this step their achievement of peace, or serenity. But, again, the experiences of these two women are different. The emphasis on feelings in working this step is illustrated in Judy's story of her first Fourth Step:

I made a list of all the nasty things I'd ever done in my entire life, even the penny bubble gum I swiped when I was three years old. I did not understand no more what a Fourth Step was than—. I showed it to [my sponsor], and she said, "This is a good sin list; you can incorporate it into your Fourth Step." Hell, I thought I'd done a Fourth Step. So I said, "I'm having so much trouble with this. How do I do it?" She said, "Sit down. Get a piece of paper. Start writing, kid. Start back at the beginning to where you can really remember, at your first real feelings, and write it out." So I started writing. After I finished writing, it was five, six, seven pages. A life history is the way I did it.

As is the case with many, for Judy the Fourth and the Fifth Steps are intimately connected:

I read it with [my sponsor]. She was sitting beside me reading this as I was reading it aloud, because I have lousy handwriting. After I gave it away to her, she did something real weird. She said, "Let's burn this sucker." I said, "Why?" She said, "I can't explain, but one of these days you'll realize why." Now of course I know.

Judy explains the connection between the unburdening and the peace that comes afterward by stating, "Writing makes you honest with yourself." She immediately modifies this assertion by denying the central role of writing in working this step: "But using a tape is the same for people who can't write. For people who can't write or are blind, they can hear themselves and say, 'Now that statement's really not true.'" What Judy seems to mean in this interesting meta-linguistic comment is that self-analysis is easier if the statements we make about ourselves have some material existence outside our-selves. Words on a page or on a tape seem somehow more real and are more easily examined than the ephemeral chunks of language that float through our minds or memories.

Even though the Mountain City women attribute the power of the Fourth Step to heal and to bring peace not to its literate mani-festation but rather to its spiritual base, Jill's fairly detailed explana-tion of the self-examination involved in the Fourth Step seems to depend in large degree on the written form. The way Jill does a Fourth Step combines Judy's life history method emphasizing feel-ings with Jennie's Big Book form. Jill explains precisely how it works for her and illustrates with a personal example:

> I write down what happened, and then I go back and look at how it affected me. I do it in a story form of what hap-pened and any feeling that I have gets written down. Then I go back and either at the bottom or on another page, I write what it affected—self-esteem, personal relationships, and all that. Then I look at how I reacted. I always try to keep that real separate, no matter what the person did to me, right or wrong, my reaction, because that's all I'm re-sponsible for. I carried for years the fact that my stepfather got mad at me and kicked me. I couldn't get over the fact that you don't kick somebody. I couldn't see what I did to deserve that. When I was able to separate what I did from the fact that it was wrong for him to kick me, then some healing came. I think it's real important that it's written

down, because I can see it right there and I can separate it. When I can separate it on the page, I can separate it inside: Here's what he did, he kicked me, and here's what I did, I started to build a wall and decide that I was going to hate him and all that stuff. I wasn't responsible for the fact that he kicked me, but I was responsible for what I decided to do. This was a real spiritual awakening.

Healing came for Jill, in addition, in writing she did for an incest-survivors group. The therapist had wanted to publish a booklet of writing by group members. Jill had been nervous about allowing her writing to be included even without her name attached. Her nervousness came from two sources: First, her awareness of the conventions of print and script and her knowledge that when she wrote this piece, those conventions were the farthest thing from her mind; and, second, her fear of revealing too much of herself in print. Her Al-Anon sponsor, who I found out only several years later was Jennie, suggested that, because I was both an English teacher and an Al-Anon member, I might be a good reader-editor-protector. One night after a meeting, Jill introduced herself and asked me to read what she written and to make corrections and suggestions. As I recall, I made neither. The piece was understated and metaphorical, too poignant, too strikingly honest for me to touch; besides, the commas were in the "right" places. During the interview two years later, Jill said of this piece: "I've healed, and I'm not in that pain anymore. My pain was on that page, and I want [the writing] back from Susan [the therapist], so I don't forget."

For Catherine, the Fourth Step was more problematic than for Tommie, Jennie, Judy, or Jill:

I would like real clarity with each step, but clarity has not been that simple for me. I would like to be able to check it off. I don't see myself as having done a Fourth Step like I hear other people say, where they wrote these things and then went to their sponsor and read all these things.

She reports that after she'd been in Al-Anon for four years, her scientist husband had gone into treatment. While he was away, the psychiatrist who had directed the departmental intervention on her husband suggested to Catherine that she complete a Fourth Step.

But she had had difficulty with the Big Book form that her sponsor advised her to follow and that the others had found helpful. What had given Catherine trouble specifically was the word *resentment:*

> I said [to my sponsor] I have things that annoy me, irritate me, bother me. See, the first column is to write down the person that I have a resentment towards. But I was like, I just don't have this. She said gently, "Just put the word *resent* down." Today it's very clear those were resentments. But it wasn't clear to me until later. Then I got to the part How It Affected My—. I could come up with, Well, it affected my self-esteem. But then it was like, so what? I didn't know what to do with it. But I kept coming to more meetings, talking to more people, kept writing. Then what happened was I had situations where I'd be irritated and bothered that kept coming up. Then it became, What in me causes me to have this reaction over and over? That's what I need to pay attention to. But with the Big Book it just was not clear.

Instead of being able to point to particular pages that constitute a Fourth Step, Catherine says that she has completed this step "in a very general way":

> I mean like writing down some feelings and then expanding on what the incident was that occurred in connection with those feelings. Or reading something in the ODAT and having a word or a sentence jump up at me and then writing on that. And talking and telling these things to other people. Not just to the same person. But I'd say a large section of it was done with my sponsor.

Lilly, who sponsors several of the women who talked to me, reports that she doesn't write much at all, that in fact she herself had difficulty writing a Fourth Step. Indeed, Lilly's experiences with the Fourth and Fifth Steps resemble Catherine's more than those of the others because for both, the writing and the talking are not clearly marked as discrete steps and because the writing seems to gain its Fourth-Step status only in the talking. Lilly's first Fourth Step was the *Blueprint.* Initially, Lilly says, she responded to the questions with a simple *Yes* or *No,* but then

> I started writing paragraphs. Each thing it asked, I started writing tons on. I even thought about tape recording it. I took a topic, like maturity, then I'd write on that. Went from too small to too big, too many words. I did a lot of free-flowing writing. I never read that to anyone. There was the thing about sharing it that bothered me.

Lilly continues her explanation of how she did her Fourth and Fifth Steps and of why the talking was significant:

> But then I began to share with others. I shared with a sponsor in Memphis. I did it in conversations. I'd talk about this that I'd written. I'd say, I wrote this. I did it in pieces. When I shared it verbally, that really changed everything. There's something about the spoken word that has always worked better for me. Maybe because I was quiet for so long. Years of quiet. Puberty to twenty-four. People wanted to know what I thought about things, and that seemed almost excruciating. So, theater made sense to me: I could do other people. I was very nervous, concerned about doing everything so perfect that I made myself sick. I was always throwing up. I really didn't think I was going to live through me. But somewhere in there I discovered talking.

All Lilly's other Fourth Steps have been "verbal"—that is, not written:

Sometimes, I'll be reading, and something will get triggered. Events with my children have triggered things. They keep me honest, how they look at you, you know. I'll think, Okay, I have to do a Fourth Step on this thing, and for weeks, things will come. I may write something down on a notecard by my bed. Then I talk to people about these things. I don't even have to identify it as a Fourth Step any more. But we'll have this conversation. It'll take two or three weeks to get to what I need to say. I always have to have the other person.

Despite her own experiences to the contrary, Lilly asks people she sponsors to write a Fourth Step because, as she puts it, the writing is "so literal." What Lilly seems to mean by *literal* is not just written but also concrete or material:

The Fourth Step is literally about looking at something. It's real important for people to feel they've literally done it so they can go past it. Some people can't write, but will do a list. Sometimes they've gotten stuck in the negative stuff. Maybe those people should write a positive list, start with a gratitude list to keep from getting stuck in shame. But it has to be literal to start. The literalness becomes symbolic. People burn them. Judy was big on burning them. Tommie needed to burn hers. I believe in literalness and people being able to see and feel what's gone from in here [she touches her chest] to out here [gesturing away from her body]. Writing does that better for most people than speaking, but not for everybody. Most people need to see it.

What these women say about writing a Fourth Step, the "searching and fearless moral inventory," and talking it out with another person in the Fifth Step makes sense intuitively. But how does this process work to heal? The unburdening or confessional use of both writing and speech is the topic of a number of studies by psychologist James W. Pennebaker and his associates when he was at Southern

Methodist University. Although most of Pennebaker's published work appears in psychology journals, his article "Self-Expressive Writing: Implications for Health, Education, and Welfare" is included in Pat Belanoff, Peter Elbow, and Sheryl Fontaine's 1991 collection on free-writing, *Nothing Begins with N: New Investigations of Freewriting*, and is a piece that should be, I think, more well known in our field than it appears to be.

In addition, Pennebaker has published a trade book, *Opening Up: The Healing Power of Confiding in Others*. In this popular book, Pennebaker says his work on confession began when he learned that it is not unusual for people taking the so-called lie-detector test to confess to crimes and then to thank the polygrapher despite knowing the confession will mean jail time. Further, after the confession, Pennebaker reports, the physical stress indicators—blood pressure, heart rate, palm perspiration—all register normal, thus making the person who confessed actually feel better. Pennebaker explains that inhibiting, holding back what one knows or has experienced, is hard work that puts stress on the body. When a person "lets go," she or he really does feel better, really does experience physiological relief. Because the polygraph information was provocative in view of his other work on body-mind relations, Pennebaker began to design systematic experiments.

In one set of experiments, which Pennebaker has carried out a number of times, a control group of undergraduates is asked to write about a something innocuous such as their dorm room or their shoes; experimental groups are asked to write about the most traumatic thing that has ever happened to them. Sometimes, the experimental groups are told to write only about their feelings, sometimes to recount only the facts of the incident but not to mention their feelings, or sometimes to write about both the facts of the incident and their feelings.

Over the next five months, students in the last group, the students who wrote about what had happened and how they felt about the incident, consistently registered about half the number of visits to the campus health center as did students in the control group or other experimental groups, a statistically significant drop. In one of these studies, blood tests showed that "those subjects who had written about their thoughts and feelings about traumatic experiences evidenced significant improvements in immune function compared with controls" ("Self-Expressive" 162). Interestingly, the facts-and-feelings group did not immediately feel better. During the days they were writing, these students reported feeling depressed. The effects, then, of confessional writing are rarely immediate as they sometimes are with the polygraph confessions but show themselves over time ("Self-Expressive" 161). After a few weeks, students in these groups reported feeling happier than students in control groups reported feeling; the facts-and-feelings group also reported having positive feelings about the experiment. Several months after the experiment itself, students in the facts-and-feelings groups also reported that writing about the incident, which in many cases they had never before disclosed, had served to help them "get past" the incident.

In another Pennebaker study, questionnaires were sent to spouses of suicide victims and spouses of fatal-accident victims. After a year, those who appeared to be "handling" the death best reported talking about the incident with friends, family, or support groups. According to Pennebaker, prayer worked as well as talking to an actual person because, he says, "prayer is a kind of disclosure" (*Opening Up* 35), an assertion Ann Ulanov and Barry Ulanov explain in detail in their book *Primary Speech: A Psychology of Prayer.* But venting emotions is not enough, Pennebaker theorizes.

Talking or writing about the facts of incident itself, not just expressing feelings about it, allows people not only to confront the trauma but also to make sense of it, Pennebaker explains. Writing decreases internal conflict because it forces structure or organization on the experience. Confessing the experience to an audience, either in writing or in speech, "forces the individual to acknowledge its existence and impact publicly." The relationship is more complex than this, however:

> Writing is beneficial, in part, because it converts the experience from images and feelings into language. The process

of coding information linguistically accomplishes several goals. First because the images and feelings are psychologically large, diffuse, and changing over time, converting them to language forces some degree of temporal organization. Further, writing, and, to a somewhat lesser degree, talking are relatively slow processes that require the sequencing of thoughts and feelings. Overwhelming images and feelings also are reduced to a surprisingly small number of concrete words. ("Self-Expressive" 166)

That is, merely putting the experience into words makes the trauma manageable. By organizing and sequencing the narrative and her feelings, the narrator gains some sense of control over what had felt uncontrollable. If this is so, then merely writing a Fourth Step should bring some amount of peace. Pennebaker hypothesizes, as well, that in disclosure to another person, people are reassured, offered help, given sympathy, admired for their resourcefulness, and given a new perspective on the event; this could almost be a description of what happens in the Fifth Step, according to reports by members of Al-Anon. Further, by the time a person writes a Fourth Step, he has become familiar with the AA and Al-Anon *disease concept* of alcoholism, which teaches family members that they did not cause the drinking, cannot control the drinking, and cannot cure the drinking. Putting one's previous experiences into words within this perspective provides a new version of reality.

The ritual of confession—which we see enacted in the Al-Anon women's Fourth Steps, in Pennebaker's subjects, and in our own students—has become so ingrained in Western culture that it has become a means to "individualization," according to Michel Foucault in *The History of Sexuality* (58). Because confession functions to form identity, we in the West have thus become, Foucault says, "a singularly confessing society" (*History* 59). Although Foucault writes specifically of confessing sexual practice, much of what he says certainly applies in the cases I take up here. The self-examination required by confession "yields . . . the basic certainties of consciousness" (*History* 60); Al-Anon members claim to arrive at insights

about themselves through the Fourth- and Fifth-Step processes. In
Al-Anon, Pennebaker's experiments, and student writing, confession is "a ritual that unfolds within a power relationship," with a
partner who can "judge, punish, forgive, console" (Foucault, *History* 61). It is "a ritual in which the expression alone, independently
of its external consequences, produces intrinsic modification in the
person who articulates it" (*History* 62). In Foucault's analysis, confession "unburdens [the confessing subject] of his wrongs, liberates
him, and promises him salvation" (*History* 62). Confession is thus
linked in our minds, according to Foucault, with freedom, a relationship he denies, seeing confession, rather, as a tool of coercion:
"the agency of domination does not reside in the one who speaks,
but in the one who listens" (*History* 62).

Foucault is right in asserting that the person listening possesses
more authority than the confessing subject, and it is certainly true
that confession has been, and can be, an instrument of control, even
torture. Nonetheless, belief in the power of confession to bring freedom, as Foucault points out, runs deep in our culture, so if people
think confession liberates, then it does, at least relatively speaking.
And relative, not absolute freedom is all there is anyway. With the
Al-Anon women, the Fourth and Fifth Steps seem to indicate, as
well, a willingness to transfer the acknowledgment of power from
one set of authorities—husbands, families, parents, even churches
—to another set, first to others who appear to have prevailed over a
common problem and then, symbolically, to a higher power. What
Foucault leaves out of his study of confession is its function in establishing intimacy. Foucault sometimes seems to write as if the
subject stands outside the social world, as if social bonds only in-
hibit the individual rather constituting her, as feminist sociologist
Dorothy Smith says in her critique of poststructuralist-postmodernist
thinkers (see appendix B as well). Although Foucault mentions the
role of confession in family or love relationships, he does not pay
much attention to its role in social bonding. Recall Tommie's comment on the Fifth Step: "It became part of sharing and trust." The
Al-Anon women who talked to me seem to see Fourth and Fifth

Steps as a means to relationship with others, with one's sponsor, and with the group.

The human impulse to language, even older than the ritual of confession that Foucault studies, is what the Al-Anon women, Pennebaker's student-subjects, and the students in our composition classes enact: the need to put what happens to us and what we feel into words, to tell others. As Lilly puts it,

> A dear friend of mine said to me, "You have to keep talking till you figure out what you're thinking and what you're feeling." I thought, That's right, I'm a talker. Then I was astounded: I understood why I was so sick. I couldn't talk. If I couldn't talk, I was going to be ill. It makes sense that some people need to write, because they aren't talkers. Some are both. Tommie is both. Jennie is a writer.

Lilly is talking here not just about preferences for linguistic encoding; she is talking about the need to communicate our experiences to other human beings, to connect with others through sharing one's thoughts and experiences.

In our culture, however, putting experience into language can be thwarted by strong prohibitions against revealing family secrets, as we see with Pennebaker's undergraduate students, who in many cases had never told anyone of the horrific events they had experienced. Families of alcoholics live under similar, though often stricter, admonitions against talking about the difficulties of their lives. Once this conflict has been resolved in favor of writing, the person begins to make sense of what seemed inchoate, to separate what is one's own actions and feelings from what is someone else's, to see even one's own emotions from a distance. As Jill explains, the separation on the page helps her to see her life as something separate from the lives of others, even from the lives of close family members. The Fifth Step also provides a new perspective: Tommie's sponsor had asked, "Is that all?" in a tone that reassured Tommie, "This is not so bad; you are not the terrible person you have feared you are."

Jennie's sponsor, as Jennie reports, "could make the connections, and she could see what everything was about" and could thereby give Jennie new information about, and a new perspective on, her private experience.

Having put their experiences into words in the Fourth Step and having been listened to in the Fifth, the Al-Anon women begin to reinterpret their lives. The sages tell us that understanding is the key to forgiveness. The Fourth Step, aided by the Fifth, brought new understanding and served thus as the beginning of healing and forgiveness for the women I interviewed. This is the beginning of the process for the Al-Anon women, not the end of it.

"I had to let go of it being perfect, and then it became perfect": Writing for Self

In the second stage of the journey, the women learn to let go of expectations of how things *ought* to be and learn to accept how things are; in Tommie's words, "I had to let go of it being perfect, and then it became perfect." Here each woman uses various literate forms to come to her own solutions to the problems in her life. It is as if once the Al-Anon women find healing or forgiveness in the Fourth and Fifth Steps, they use other written forms to find freedom, to get past the disease into "ease," as Lilly phrases it. In this stage, the main genre appears to be the journal, but there are others. Several of the women I interviewed are journal writers, though none writes every day and only Catherine follows a strict form. Interestingly, some use other terms for this writing: Jennie writes "in my steno pad" and Catherine "in my spiral notebook." Again, as with the Fourth Step, their experiences with journals are different.

Tommie traces the evolution of her journal:

> I started writing, keeping journals, in October of '83, before I came to the program in March of '84. I started writing because people couldn't listen to me any more. I wrote as release and analysis, all in one. This notebook was for

recipes, music, kids' notes. There's a lot of Dear God Letters and prose.

The Dear God Letters began, she says, after she read Alice Walker's novel *The Color Purple:* "To me, my journal is writing to God. If Celie could do it, I could do it."

For the pieces Tommie calls prose, teachers of literature would use the term poetry. Read aloud, they sound like poetry; on the page, they look like poetry. But, according to Tommie, "Prose doesn't rhyme. It has meter, but it doesn't rhyme. Poetry rhymes." When I ask for more explanation, she shares an example: "I wrote this early, in my disease. This is before I came to recovery, when I was hitting bottom. There's disease there, but there was also great health there I didn't know I had":

October 2, 1983.
Get up kids. Mom slept in.
Hurry up so you won't be late for school.
Had this happened before?
Yes, only just yesterday and the day before.
Was it happening again? Yes, it was.
Why? Why?
Such a small question that seems to require a large
      assortment of even larger and longer answers.
Every year of her life Why had different answers.
Oh, they were easy to explain away at first,
and there was never a worry or a sinking feeling in the pit
      of her stomach.
But it seemed to be getting worse.
It took days to answer.
Days that dragged on into weeks.
"Well," she said aloud, "if you hadn't stayed up half the
      night you wouldn't have slept in."
That was easy. But why did you stay up half the night?
The last half of the evening your eyelids banged against

your brain trying to stay awake.
The house became irritatingly quiet.
You were wide awake, every inch of your brain crawling with
        all of its vast knowledge.
You've heard that knowledge is a good thing,
but you don't feel good.
As a matter of fact, you feel lousy.
Take away *u* and *y,* add a *t,* and lousy becomes lost.
Somehow they seem to mean the same thing.
And the worst part is that this feeling seems
to be governed by everyone else.
You can't seem to grasp it in your hands and take control.
Your mind wants to, so why doesn't it?
Aha! There's Why again.
So easy to answer for the world,
yet so difficult on a first-name basis.
Maybe that's it—anonymity. Then nobody knows you.
Not even Why will know you.
Every land on this earth has works of art, literature, music
        and monuments written by and dedicated to the unknown.
Wrong. The world seeks out the unknowns.
You don't want to justify yourself to the world, only to
        yourself.
So back to square one again.
Well, let's take a look at this situation.
Mirror, mirror on the wall. You ain't got no sense at all.
Snow White is a fairy tale. Poison apples don't put me to
        sleep, Why does.
And it keeps me wide awake, too,
Just trying to come up with any answer that doesn't cause my
        tired brain to think, "But why?"
I know. I'll eliminate Why from my vocabulary,
Replace it with a suitable word.
Let's see. Enough: too restricting and confining and final.
Okay: too easy.
Mom. She doesn't live your life.

Daddy? Out of reach.
World. Full of static, absolutely no feedback.
Walls. Only echoes.
Husband. Searching too?
Kids. Unfair choice, you had your childhood. Let them have
    theirs.
So, I guess it's you and me.
Hello, Why.
You have enlightened me, given me knowledge to expand myself
    and restrict myself.
You are a never-answered question, running into you as I
    turn around every unexplored corner.
You're self-analytical and egotistical, degrading and
    uplifting, boring and open-minded.
Let's be friends. Okay?
Gee, I hope I don't sleep in tomorrow morning.

For Tommie, the journal is very much a means of claiming
ownership of her life: "I write the journal for me. It's not an assignment." At the same time, however, Tommie believes that sharing her
journal is a way of sharing her spiritual growth:

> I tell other people in the program that part of my recovery
> is keeping a journal. I write for me, but when I show it to
> you, it helps you. I show my journal to people I'm talking
> to. Even with some Dear God letters not being finished
> 'cause sometimes I fell asleep writing them. The perfection
> of it isn't the point. See, I had to let go of it being perfect,
> and then it became perfect. If I'da done it the way I thought
> you had to do it, I'da never done it.

Tommie says that she does not write in her journal every day
but typically every other day, sometimes only a sentence or two.
These days, she says, the journal is a choice, but early on in her
recovery, it was a "have-to":

That's why I believe in journals. You don't have to know
what to write; just pick up the pen, even if all you write is
the date. It was a great tool for me. It's a reaching for something outside of you. Sometimes it would end up as a poem
or prose. And I call that a form of meditation. A thought;
then, this feels important. So I'd write it down, and I'd start
to see what it was about. It would just evolve. That's how
poetry—and writing—comes about. You have an original
thought, and you expand on it. But I can't expand on it today by thinking about it. I have to let it be. It'll come, but
I can't force it. If I wanted to force it, I could go to school
and take classes.

Jennifer doesn't use the term *journal,* even though informal private writing seems to function for her in same way that the journal
does for Tommie. In fact, Jen says with certainty, "I don't keep a
journal or diaries. But I have. Once, when my sponsor went out of
town. Once, when my husband was in treatment. It was a way of
recording what went on." Nonetheless, Jennie talks about the writing she does "in my steno pad," where she composes letters she
does not intend to mail, records dreams and analyzes them, defines
words, and freewrites about issues in her life in order to attain
clarity or find connections.

Just as Tommie uses the Dear God letters in her journal as a
way to attain emotional detachment from the problems in her life,
so Jennie uses her God Can notes. This practice started for Jennie
with an actual can in her kitchen—Folger's coffee, I think—that had
pasted on it a label declaring "I Can't. God Can." Jennie explains
how this works:

Some people can visualize putting people in God's hands,
and that does it for them. Well, it doesn't do it for me. I
have to write it down and put it in my God Can to get rid
of it. I try to condense it into as few words as possible, a
tiny slip of paper. It may be an inch or two inches long—I
have one that's probably about three inches long—about

half an inch wide. Now I have two God Cans. One is actually a mahogany butterfly someone gave me.

Here the written text becomes for Jen symbolic of the problem, and
only when the paper is put away can she put the problem out of her
mind. The process is similar to Judy's written Fourth-Step inventory,
which was burned after she had used it in her Fifth-Step confession
with her sponsor.

Among Mountain City Al-Anon members, the God Can is not
exclusive to Jennie; at meetings and with people she sponsors, she
has shared this technique for finding freedom from some problem:

There is a release when I write and put it in my God Can.
It seems more concrete. So when I have a real difficult
time, then I write my prayers because it is more concrete.
And I have written things, pages, and folded them up and
put the pages in the God Can. It's almost like a catharsis.

Judy touches on this sense of writing as release when she explains what she writes and under what circumstance: "It may be
piddly stuff, it may be something big. But when I get angry, I write
like hell. And I just keep on writing until I get tired and I'm not mad
anymore." Once, when she was working through what she calls "the
grief bit, the heavy duty stuff," she wrote, she says, with her mind
going faster than she could write until three o'clock in the morning.
When her husband got up to see what was wrong, Judy gave him
the pages to read so that he would know what she was feeling.

Besides emotional release, Judy's everyday writing often has a
domestic function. On a pad by the telephone in the kitchen, Judy
writes notes to herself, not just for her own state of mind but for her
husband's benefit as well: "I write 'Have a Nice Day' or 'Be Happy.'
That lets me know that it's a good day or I'm having a happy day. Or
if I'm downstairs and Jack comes in, he knows what kind of mood
I'm in." She explains why communicating her upbeat moods is important:

> See, when he was drinking, he never knew when he came
> home if I was going to kill him or not. I was hot and
> cold. If he wasn't home when I thought he should be, I'd
> rearrange all the living room furniture and turn the lights
> out, so when he came in, he'd fall. I kept thinking in my
> mind, if he falls down, he'll quit drinking.

These notes seem informational for her husband but persuasive for
Judy herself.

Jill also tells of writing to her husband but not to reassure him.
She wrote, she reports, "this wonderfully angry letter. I [just] reread
it, and it's great." Jill left it on her husband's pillow but retrieved it
three or four hours later, before he came home: "I realized I didn't
need to have him read it. But I told him about it. And I said, 'Some-
day I'm going to let you read it.'"

Like Jennie, Catherine doesn't use the word *journal* for her
ongoing personal writing. Instead, Catherine writes "in my spiral
notebook": "I remember clearly the first thing I wrote in the notebook was I recopied some notes at the Al-Anon conference I was
attending. I didn't know how to start, so I wrote, 'I need to begin.'"
Despite her education, writing as part of her Al-Anon program has
been difficult for Catherine:

> Early on, I tried using that list of feelings, and if there was
> an incident that came up, I would try to write down the
> feeling I had. To come up with words for what I was feeling
> was real difficult, but as I went down that list, words would
> pop out. I didn't know the names for feelings because,
> growing up, I don't think I even knew about that part of my
> life. I'm sure it was there. It's part of being human. But rules
> like "Don't talk back" and "Children are to be seen and not
> heard" didn't allow for much encouraging expression.

Despite such inhibitions, Catherine has found that writing in
her spiral notebook is necessary for her peace of mind:

I know that for me when I don't do writing on a regular basis, I get off into my version of the world, this frantic wanting to do this activity and that, and take care of clutter. I lose my serenity, my connection to my higher power. The written word there is very important. An issue never seems to be as intense after I write. If I write about it, it's not as big. There comes a lot more clarity when I write.

Catherine's sense that writing brings clarity is reiterated in something Lilly said about a woman she sponsors but did not name:

When she'd move away from writing her journal, she'd be different. So I'd say, "I'd like you writing in your journal. There seems to be an enormous benefit in writing your journal." She'd say, "I haven't done that in a week." And I'd say, "I can tell, because you feel very different." Things got less clear [when she wasn't writing]. For her, writing was real important and that there be a consistency to it. That was a process she needed. But she's the only person I recommended that to. It was more important than she realized.

Catherine is precise with her spiral notebooks in ways that the other women do not seem to be with their journals. For example, Catherine begins each entry on a separate page, recording date, day, year, and exact time. By the time of the interviews, she had filled, she thought, at least ten notebooks. Further, Catherine is the only one of the women who talks about editing as she writes. She does so, she says, because

I have been very much aware that someone else may read them some day, if I died. I have been concerned about trying to be specific on occasion in case someone should read it, and I have been specifically not specific at other times in case someone would read it. I have used some names, like I've written *Beth*. But I've written other things without names.

Like the other Al-Anon women, Catherine has learned to value the sharing: "We can learn from one another's strengths. To withhold that is really sad. So in a sense I wouldn't mind other people reading my notebooks. In fact, I've almost thought that I don't want them destroyed. It's like I've worked hard. They are a record of my journey." Catherine's concern for the anonymity of the people she writes about and her careful dating of each entry indicate self-consciousness about the permanence of writing and the possibility of an audience other than herself.

Among the Mountain City women, others also see their journals as a record of their growth. Though Judy's informal writing at this stage is less structured than, say, Tommie's, Judy has kept everything she's written as part of her program, and these writings function as a record of her progress: "I've dated them so I can go back and look at them and know where I was at that point in time. I go back and read them." Jill says that her journal is a record of who she was. After I called to make an appointment for the interview, Jill went through her writing, looking at "some of the things I hadn't read since I'd written them. And my emotions were there. I like seeing me down there [on the page]. It makes me real."

Like Tommie, Jill had started writing before she came into the program. The earliest pages of her journal, she says, contain passages of scripture and written prayers. Before her involvement with Al-Anon and during the worst of her husband's drinking, Jill had become involved in a local church. She was, she says, "looking for something to help me because I was in pretty bad shape." But for a variety reasons, the church did not prove helpful for Jill. Despite being "very focused on prayer and doing the right thing and going to church" she was, she says, still having "living problems." The message Jill says she got from the members of this congregation was simply to "let go and let God," advice that seemed impossible to her at the time:

> Man, I couldn't do that. It went against everything I had
> ever—. As a child in order to survive what I went through,
> I had to feel some sense of control, or I would have died

somewhere inside. So when someone said, "Just let go and let God," without giving me some other way to focus, I just couldn't do it.

She had felt guilty, she says, for being unable to follow these precepts. Later, after becoming associated with Al-Anon, she had considered the church's teachings simplistic and naive and had thus felt ashamed about that period of her life. Interestingly, however, at the time of the interview, Jill's response to her earliest journal writing with its prayers and scripture was positive: "When I went back and saw this stuff, even in terms of the stuff I wrote that's so religious, I don't have shame for that any more. That was me then." The Fourth-Step writing was the process by which Jill was able, in Al-Anon, to "let go and let God."

Lilly talks, too, about the record-keeping function of a journal. Though she herself does not regularly keep a journal as part of her Al-Anon program, she did keep one after her older son was born:

> It was the most incredible thing to read when I was going through forgiveness about what kind of parent I was the first three or four years of his life, when I was so crazed trying to control this addict. All I remembered was what I'd done wrong. I couldn't remember any joy, except his birth. When I went back and read this journal, it was full of all the fun. The journal gave me that back, because I'd written it down. It helped me forgive myself.

In this middle stage, these women devise various literate strategies for coming to terms with their experiences, dealing with their emotions, reassessing other people's rules and cultural expectations, and accepting the unchangeable conditions of their lives— in short, for letting go of their own private struggles. They use their writing to chart, record, analyze, accept, and change their emotions and their lives. Using various written forms—prose, Dear God letters, journals, God Can notes, and letters—these women are, as Robert Brooke would say, negotiating their own identities.

In his book *Writing and Sense of Self: Identity Negotiation in Writing Workshops,* Brooke draws on social psychology, the political and cultural theories of leftist educators and feminists, and interpretive anthropology to show that for some people in some particular situations writing is a way to form and re-form the self. Denying the possibility of the self as an essential "little me" with a "fixed consciousness that never changes" (15), Brooke argues that individuals "construct their particular sense of self from the competing social definitions of self which surround them" (4). These competing definitions set off internal conflicts that Brooke claims students can resolve through the writing they do in writing workshops. Anne J. Herrington and Marcia Curtis offer rich examples of this phenomenon in their recent book *Persons in Progress: Four Stories of Writing and Personal Development in College,* a report of longitudinal studies of writing across four students' entire undergraduate careers. Though Brooke's and Herrington and Curtis's focus is on students in college writing classes and not on adults in self-help programs, it is useful to consider the journals and other informal writing of the Al-Anon women with Brooke's notions in mind.

Because the women I interviewed have deliberately chosen to analyze their lives and have consciously constructed new ways of believing and acting, they would, I am convinced, agree with Brooke's assertion the self is not an unchanging "little me" but rather a more fluid entity that negotiates among the claims of competing groups. Defining *identity* as "what is most central or important about the self" and *negotiations* as "attempts to mitigate the clash between opposing forces, to compromise between conflicting camps, to satisfy groups with different demands" (12), Brooke says that writing can be "one aspect of identity negotiation, one way that people can negotiate how they view themselves and how they want others to view them within the complex interactions of contemporary society" (6).

This seems an apt description of the what the Al-Anon women do in this stage of their journey. The women I interviewed seem to be trying to find what they think is most important, most central, about who they are, as they consciously search among the conflicting demands of various cultural roles: from traditional notions of the role of the good woman or good wife—silent, obedient, and passive—to more recent models of women—solving problems, making decisions, and participating actively in their own lives. One set of conflicts they are negotiating includes the one between the ideal of the always-calm-and-perfect-mother and the reality of old family models of anger or violence. They move among religious teachings that vary from pictures of God as an exacting and distant scorekeeper punishing people who fail (especially women who can't keep their husbands sober) to gentler images of a higher power as an approachable and benign presence providing help for people who ask to more agnostic notions of a collective unconscious or inner conscience. Children, spouses, parents, siblings, bosses, supervisors, fellow employees, churches, friends, neighbors, community groups, therapists and therapy groups, alcohol-treatment professionals, Al-Anon literature, Al-Anon meetings, Al-Anon sponsors, and other program friends—all these and more offer competing definitions of self to these women. As they change their alignment within this constellation of competing entities, their identities change. Just as Brooke's college students negotiate their identities through the writing they do in writing workshops, so, too, my research participants negotiate their identities through the writing they do as part of their Al-Anon program.

For the students in Brooke's study of college composition classes, "writing is a symptom of group membership" (8). Certainly this seems true, as well, for the women I interviewed. Indeed group membership—not just the Al-Anon philosophy—is a major attraction of Al-Anon. It is not unusual, for example, to hear in meetings that Al-Anon members "kept coming back" because they felt comfortable with the group or because they admired the people they met there. Judy, for example, says of her very first Al-Anon meeting: "The lady who chaired that meeting was so damn serene. She even chewed her chewing gum serenely. She was cool as a cucumber. And I had to have that coolness." Being part of the group means working the program means writing. Al-Anon in general encourages writing—for example, the *Blueprint,* not to mention countless references in the official literature to writing Fourth Steps or Eighth

Steps. The Al-Anon community in Mountain City in particular talks explicitly about writing as a way to achieve peace or as a strategy to deal with problems. In this community of women, then, writing brings them into relationship with each other, becoming indeed "a symptom of group membership."

Part of the identity negotiation among the Mountain City women includes rereading their previous writing. Rather than seeing previous selves as sources of internal conflict, the women see—or come to see—those earlier versions of themselves with compassion and thus learn to accept their own histories. They see where they have come from, and they measure their progress from those earlier times. Though Jill has moved away from the church she was part of before Al-Anon, she honors who she was when she searched there for help from her pain. She uses her writing to track her identity and to accept herself at various stages on her journey: "I could remember me being there. I could remember how I felt and why I wrote and know that I could grieve for the person that was there, that me that was there. And I could feel wonderful that my higher power had brought me through that." Tommie would say that when Jill let go of the notion of being perfect, she became perfect. For the Mountain City women, literacy becomes a means for fostering an ongoing reflective examination of self in relation to others. And thus the women reach the third stage in their journey.

"We can't carry our message if we don't have our own language": Coming to Voice

As the Mountain City Al-Anon women use writing to heal and to negotiate identity, they seem to develop, in addition, a voice—that is to say, the confidence to use language to take a stand. Although all the women who talked to me seem aware of the power of language, Tommie worked particularly hard in the interview to explain the capacity of language to heal and to liberate. For Tommie, healing and liberation from the past come in and through language: "In [Steps] Six and Seven, you get your own language. See, we can't carry our message if we don't have our own language," she says, referring to Step Six, which reads, "Were entirely ready to have God remove all these defects of character," and Step Seven, which says, "Humbly asked Him to remove our shortcomings." With her reference to Step Twelve—"Having had a spiritual awakening as a result of these steps, we tried to carry this message to others, and to practice these principles in all our affairs"—Tommie seems to mean that having asked for a change in their own lives, people who practice the Twelve Steps are then able to take the message of healing to others.

To illustrate what she means by getting one's own language, Tommie tells a number of stories. One is of a physical fight between her husband and her teenaged son that occurred about the time of her Sixth and Seventh Steps:

> I couldn't move. I couldn't get in between them. But my words came. I remembered, "You have your words, Tommie. Use your words, Tommie." So I screamed to my husband, "Remember you're the adult," and he took his hands off our son. I was amazed at the power of my words.

As she elaborates on the concept of getting one's own language, Tommie tells of a woman in the Mountain City Al-Anon program who writes down what people say in meetings if she believes that their words contain a spiritual truth she needs to know. When this woman comes to talk with Tommie, she wants to write down what Tommie says. But, Tommie explains,

> I told her I don't want her writing down anything I say any more. I feel now in her relationship with me that she's moving to her own language. If she is to remember what I've said, she'll tell it back to me, and it won't even be the same thing I've said because she will have been added to it. I don't want to hear my language from her any more. I want to hear hers. And I'm starting to hear it. I can sense that she's moving to her own language.

Finally, Tommie tells the story of a woman at a meeting in New York City, when Tommie had gone there with Lilly. This woman, Tommie says, described herself before coming to the program as "a parrot" because she had, she said, endlessly repeated what all the authorities in her life had told her. Celebrating this other woman's transformation, Tommie explains, "She has come to her own language," a term strikingly similar to bell hooks's much-quoted phrase "coming to voice," a phenomenon that hooks regards in her book *Talking Back: Thinking Feminist, Thinking Black* as a "metaphor for self-transformation" (12).

Finding one's own language in Steps Six and Seven ["Were entirely ready to have God remove all these defects of character"; "Humbly asked Him to remove our shortcomings"] is not just Tommie's experience. Catherine recounts this story of "coming to voice":

> I felt like I was maybe at Step Five, Six, or Seven. I went back to see the same priest I'd done the Third Step prayer with. I went to see the priest the second time, not being exactly sure where I was on the steps. So I went and talked with Father and did the Seventh Step there. When I came home [that day], I wrote in my spiral notebook like I'd never written before. It was as if my husband were in front of me, and I was lamming into him. Anger kinds of things. To me, it was almost like maybe God had removed one of those shortcomings, and I was able to express anger. It was so dramatic. Later I felt somewhat bad and guilty about this kind of writing. But my sponsor said it was mine.

Catherine supplies a more recent example in an account of a phone conversation she'd had with her estranged husband. At a particularly abrupt response from him, she responded, she says, in a way that was unlike her: "That's where once I'd have shut down. But I said, 'Paul, I'm trying to tell you something about me.' I think he finally realized. I just want to be able to speak up. I just want to get the words out."

Though she does not make explicit connections to Steps Six and Seven, Judy came to voice, so to speak, writing for the wider, national Al-Anon community. As Judy tells the story, she had spent many months mourning the death of an older woman she had met through the program, a woman she refers to as Momma because "All my life I've always adopted parents. Momma and Poppa are the only ones who ever adopted me back." After using the program to deal with her grief, Judy saw in an Al-Anon newsletter a call for members to write their stories for a book on getting through difficult situations. Her response was a three-page essay, which she asked me to proofread. Two years later, during the time of the interviews, Judy believed her piece would not be included in the book because a more recent description of the proposed book seemed no longer to fit the experience she had written about. Yet Judy expressed confidence in her message: "I still think it would help other people because grief is a big deal. I think everybody who goes through grief, whether it be from a death or grieving all kinds of different things, they go through what I went through, and I think it will help." Judy's essay, though edited for length, is indeed in the 1990 Al-Anon volume *In All Our Affairs: Making Crises Work for You.*

For academic readers who publish regularly, Judy's publication of a short essay may not seem impressive. But as Judy told me when she called to ask for editing help and as she reiterated in the interview, she is—in her own words—"only a high-school graduate." Judy does not claim to be a writer. She does not talk, as Jill does, about writing "wonderfully morose poetry" when she was sixteen, or recall, as Lilly does, writing "intense analytical" college papers. Judy says:

> Writing is pretty important to me, but like I asked you to proofread that for me and change the grammar and punctuation and all that, because it's been twenty years since I've been in school. I would not have sent that to World Service without it being proofread and done properly. You

didn't change my story or the meaning. But I'm quite illiterate in that sense. It's been twenty years.

Despite her doubt about her mastery of the official language of print and her sense of public writing as strictly following those standards, Judy had a message to carry. With help from her Al-Anon community and with her Al-Anon tools, she had come through a debilitating grief that threatened to turn into a full-blown depression. Remembering the admonition to share her "experience, strength, and hope," Judy saw this part of her life as a significant experience that could help someone else. So, she wrote the piece for a public audience and did what needed to be done to send it to an organization whose publications are read by many thousands. Convinced of the validity of her message, Judy used her own language to share her message.

Finally, Jennifer also finds a voice for her message. Despite writing Fourth Steps, God Can notes, and various kinds of meditations in her steno pad, Jennie did not, in 1990, think of herself as a writer: "I've not gotten back into writing. I think it's sorta like I've had writer's block for years. I wrote a lot when I was younger. I wrote a lot of poetry. I'm hoping I'll get that back. I remember writing as a teenager. I liked writing then." Yet she admits that in recent years, "I've written one poem that had to do with fear. And I did do some writing when I took that short-story class." The short-story class offered through the local arts center was taught, I add, by a prize-winning fiction writer. It is interesting, I think, to consider that Jennie implicitly defines the term *writing* as only creative or imaginative writing, denying herself the title writer, despite writing on a daily basis for several years.

When I interviewed Jennie, most of her writing was for the classes she was taking. Returning to graduate school after an hiatus of ten years probably accounts at least partially for the initial difficulty Jennie reported in writing her school papers. Halfway through her masters program, Jennie found her writing becoming easier and better because she now was able to claim authorship of school assignments in a way she had not done previously:

There's a different part of me that produces what it is I need
to write. Like this morning, I had to do this reaction paper
on reality therapy. You have to react to what you like, what
you don't like, about the book. But this other part of me
says, "Wait a minute, this is what you believe." So I talked
about how I believe people have a preference in how they
operate: thinking mode, doing mode, and feeling mode.
That some people, if they prefer just one, then they have
less of the other two. Sometimes you can have none of one
or both. I made it personal: How I operated when I was
younger was more of a doing mode. Then it was a thinking
mode and there were no feelings, and I paid less attention
to the doing mode. Now it's more on a feeling level, the
thinking and the doing are less important. But there seems
to be coming a balance. I seem to be moving toward a balance.

Jennie goes on to explain that she is unaccustomed to self-
disclosure in a school paper:

This is not normally what I'd put in a class paper. There's
something in me that's different, that's putting together
what I want to say and comes out with it. I had an idea of
which way I wanted to go with this paper, but when it
came to sitting down and writing it, it came from somewhere else. It's not like what I wanted to write, what I
thought I was going to write. What I did was more integrated and at a higher level intellectually. I need to relax
and let that part of me come out.

So for Jennie, then, even her academic writing has a spiritual
aspect. Her writing, she says, is often

something that comes from somewhere within me. Like
last night, I was up reading this reality therapy stuff, trying
to get it finished, and just all of a sudden came those words

"I believe." So I grabbed a deposit slip and I wrote on the side of it so when I got up in the morning I could use it in my paper. It feels like it's—in me—but from somewhere other than my thinking.

In discovering this something that comes from somewhere other than her thinking, Jennie is learning to trust her own power with language, a power that is both generative and freeing.

Speaking up, sharing one's message, getting one's own language —these are examples of what hooks, in *Talking Back*, calls "coming to voice," a phrase she defines as "moving from silence into speech" and identifies as a "revolutionary gesture . . . especially relevant for women who are speaking and writing for the first time." This "metaphor for self-transformation" is, she says, "a rite of passage where one moves from being object to being subject" (12). For some women, speaking their truth about their experiences, fears, hopes, or desires is indeed a revolutionary gesture. For the wife of an alcoholic, the move from silence to speech can indicate her transformation from object to subject.

Catherine may be the most dramatic example. When she came to Al-Anon, as we have heard, Catherine had difficulty even naming her own feelings. After the Seventh Step ("Humbly asked Him to remove our shortcomings"), she was able to use language to express long repressed anger toward her husband; what is more, she could interpret this expression of anger, which childhood training had taught her was wrong, as the sign of the removal of a shortcoming. And for Catherine to say aloud to her husband "Paul, I am trying to tell you something about me" is literally a move from silence to speech. Recall Lilly's comment: "I understood why I was so sick. I couldn't talk. If I couldn't talk, I was going to be ill." This same impulse is what Audre Lorde is talking about in "The Transformation of Silence into Language and Action:" "I have come to believe over and over that what is most important to me must be spoken, made verbal and shared, even at the risk of having it bruised or misunderstood. That the speaking profits me, beyond any other effect" (40).

Coming to voice is, hooks says, "for the oppressed, the colonized, the exploited, and those who stand and struggle side by side a gesture of defiance that heals, that makes new life and new growth possible" (*Talking Back* 9). The women I interviewed do not suffer Third World oppression. They are not disenfranchised. Only Tommie would be classified as economically disadvantaged, though even as part of the working poor, Tommie and her family have the basic necessities and a few luxuries. The women I interviewed do not see themselves as victims. Nonetheless, despite their mostly middle-class status, the women who talked with me came of age in a world where patriarchy was the organizing principle, where female roles were stringently enforced, where women had little power, where women's voices routinely went unheard, where women's thoughts and desires went unsaid. If Jean Baker Miller's depiction of domination and subordination is accurate (esp. 3–12), then the culture these women grew up in trained them to take a secondary position not only in their families of origin but also in their marriages. It trained them for silence —and for alienation from their own needs.

Alcoholism exacerbates this situation. Active alcoholics of both sexes often exert their will on their families by any means necessary, including withdrawal, temper tantrums, or violence or threats of it. As an Al-Anon member once succinctly explained, "Active alcoholics don't have relationships, they take hostages." When alcoholism combines with male privilege, family members not only suffer but often do so in silence. Some of my research participants were clearly exploited from within their own families: The sexual abuse of Jill by her grandfather and the physical abuse of Tommie by her stepfather are extreme examples. If the personal is political, as many believe, then when women use language to speak against domestic oppression, to express dissatisfaction, to give voice to desires separate from families' or husbands', to articulate different beliefs, when they use language to change themselves and their environment, it is a revolutionary gesture. While Foucault is right to point to the coercive use of confession, that is not its only function. For the

Mountain City women—and women may be the key word here—confession, in the form of Fourth Steps or journals within a supportive environment, is practice for speaking out.

"Writing as an avenue to special kind of power": *Becoming the Subject*

Critics of Twelve-Step programs, such as Wendy Kaminer, argue that the recovery movement is actually a manifestation of political conservatism because it privatizes social problems. There is some justification in this charge. Instead of social analysis, which might supply an awareness of systemic injustice and in turn lead to public activism, Twelve-Step programs focus on the individual or on the family. It is true, for example, that much Al-Anon literature assumes rather than critiques the traditional role of wife in our culture. Yet Kaminer and other critics seem to think that social change can begin only with a public declaration of a political agenda. Offering a more complex view of how change occurs, hooks argues, in *Sisters of the Yam: Black Women and Self-Recovery,* that focus on the self may be a necessary first step in arriving at social activism. She says that critical examination of painful life experiences allows for understanding of not only what happened but why; it is this *why* that often includes the social conditions that are beyond any individual's power to change, she argues. Understanding these conditions can bring compassion for the persons who inflicted harm. Compassion is a significant step in coming to grips with one's agency, according to hooks: "Our capacity to forgive always allows us to be in touch with our own agency (that is, the power to act on our own behalf to change a situation). . . . Without agency, we collapse into passivity, inertia, depression, and despair" (167).

In *Sisters of the Yam,* hooks explains that those who want to politicize movements for self-recovery have found that participants often "felt that they did not have time for political work because they felt there were so many things messed up in their psyches, or in their daily lives, that they were just barely keeping a hold on life"

(5). hooks writes that she has come to understand that sometimes the personal must take precedence over the political:

> For some time now . . . I have seen that we cannot fully create effective movements for social change if individuals struggling for that change are not also self-actualized or working towards that end. When wounded individuals come together in groups to make change our collective struggle is often undermined by all that has not been dealt with emotionally. (4–5)

In other words, the emotional health of the individuals involved may be necessary to the good health of political movements.

Cornel West posits a similar order in an essay called "Nihilism in Black America": spiritual awareness, then political activism. West recommends as an antidote to the feelings of hopelessness of many African Americans, especially those in the inner cities, what he calls a "politics of conversion." People need to believe, he says, "that there is hope for the future and meaning to the struggle" (18). West goes on to explain that the kind of genuine social change he calls for "rests neither on an agreement about what justice consists of nor on an analysis of how racism, sexism, or class subordination operates" (18–19). Defining nihilism as "a disease of the soul" (18) and comparing it to alcoholism and drug addiction, West asserts that this sickness "is not overcome by arguments or analyses. . . . Any disease of the soul must be conquered by a turning of one's soul. This turning is done through one's own affirmation of one's worth—an affirmation fueled by the concern of others" (18–19).

Though all the Mountain City women who talked with me are white and have thus not been subject to the racism that both hooks and West are writing about, they have been the recipients of a sexism that is also a virulent social evil. Sexism, too, destroys souls by teaching women that they are lesser human beings. At this stage of their lives, my Al-Anon research participants are "turning their souls." Writing and talking, they affirm their own and one another's worth.

What hooks is talking about in *Talking Back* as well as what my research participants both talk about and illustrate is using language, both written and spoken, to name and claim one's life. Both hooks and the Al-Anon women who spoke with me are talking about the process by which one can achieve agency, can become the subject in one's own narrative. This is, in short, empowerment, a term much overused these days but appropriate in this context. Perhaps it is possible to theorize that at the intersection of literacy and spirituality, we find power. Years ago, William Coles explained:

> I value [writing] as a form of language using, language using understood as the primary means by which all of us run order through chaos, thereby giving ourselves the identities we have. . . . Thus I have a way of offering writing as an avenue to a special kind of power, the only power I know that is uncorrupting and that for my money it therefore makes any sense to have: the power to choose with awareness, to change and adapt consciously, and in this sense to be able to have a share in determining one's own destiny. (253)

When scholars in rhetoric and composition discuss writing and power, they most often mean economic or political power first, intellectual or social power second—power over others. Perhaps it is time for us to include spiritual power. It is time for us to see all the multifaceted ways actual human beings use literacy to compose power in their daily lives.

3 / Reading as a Matter of Life

When I began this study, my goal was to verify my sense that people at the end of the twentieth century, like those in untold centuries before, can have spiritual motives for their literate practice. My hypothesis was confirmed by the first round of interviews with the Mountain City Al-Anon women. But just as the writing of the women who talked with me was a great deal more complicated than simply writing for spiritual purposes, their reading turns out to be more complex than I had thought it would be. The reports of their reading show, as did the stories of their writing, that for the Mountain City Al-Anon women, there is no decontextualized literacy, no dichotomy between orality and literacy, no reading or writing separated from talk. For the women I talked with, what the text says changes over time, as the reader changes, and reading is both an individual and a communal activity.

The point of their reading is to see—to find—a relationship between the text and their lives. The books the women read, as Kenneth Burke puts it in "Literature as Equipment for Living," "name typical, recurrent situations" (293) and have "direct bearing . . . upon matters of welfare" (296). The women read for what Burke has called "strategies" or "attitudes," for "equipments for living" (304). They show a marked preference for "aesthetic," or experiential, reading over "efferent," or informational, reading, stances Louise M. Rosenblatt describes in *The Reader, the Text, and the Poem: The Transactional Theory of the Literary Work*. This notion is important, I think, because until quite recently, most studies of reading have assumed efferent reading to be the norm, setting up academic ways of reading as the ultimate goal for reading.

The women I talked to have always been readers, but their reading has taken on some different roles as they have come to

Al-Anon and to this particular group, where reading is a conscious and intentional activity. As I have indicated already, at Al-Anon meetings and in private conversations, exhortations to "read the literature" are common. The typical opening ritual for Al-Anon meetings includes reading aloud several Al-Anon texts. Unless the meeting focuses specifically on the steps, the main part of an Al-Anon meeting is often discussion of readings in *One Day at a Time in Al-Anon* (the ODAT) or some other Al-Anon publication. The women who talked with me generally read the ODAT every day. In addition to reading Al-Anon literature, my informants also read or have read other books about alcoholism and about families of alcoholics. They read nonprogram meditation books, some of which are directed specifically to "recovering" persons, others of which are religious in origin or focus, like *The Upper Room,* a devotional booklet published by the United Methodist Church, or books by Anthony De Mello, a Jesuit writer. They read writers on spirituality like Thomas Merton and Hugh Prather. They read novels: detective stories by Robert B. Parker and Tony Hillerman and fictional narratives about women who survive adversity by Toni Morrison and Alice Walker. They read the poetry of Ntozake Shange. They read other popular forms: magazines, newspapers, biographies, romances, mysteries, science fiction, true crime. At the time of the interviews, Jennifer and Jill had returned to the university and so were reading, in their words, "tons" of academic articles and books.

During the interviews when I asked initially, "What do you read?", the replies ranged from genres to topics to quantities. Jennifer said she was reading "twenty-four hours a day," mostly school texts for her masters program in counseling. At the time of the interview, she was reading rational emotive therapy and reality therapy. Jill, who reads "an awful, awful lot," said that she was on a "murder mystery kick," in addition to the reading attribution theory as part of her summer job as a research assistant in social work. Catherine replied that she read the local paper and *Time.* She reported that before the separation from her husband, she had liked reading *Sports Illustrated* because of the caliber of the writing. Both Judy and Jill read *People,* and Jill is a regular reader of *Good House-*

keeping. Jen says she gets the local Sunday paper but no longer subscribes to magazines because of the expense. Similarly, Tommie says, "I can't afford newspapers and magazines. I would love to, but that's not a priority. These are a luxury. The money is needed to maintain the home and put food on the table. I get magazines from other people. People share with me." Tommie goes on to explain how she feels about borrowing reading material: "This was shame for me, that I couldn't afford it. But finally I couldn't care any more. I'm not ashamed any more. Now I can ask somebody if they have something I could read."

When asked "What program things do you read?", the women responded with replies that included not only Al-Anon and AA material but also the commercially published meditation books. The texts they read on a daily basis or with some regularity include *One Day at a Time* (ODAT), *Alateen: A Day at a Time,* and *As We Understood,* all published by Al-Anon; *Alcoholics Anonymous* (the AA Big Book) and AA's *Twelve Steps and Twelve Traditions* (the AA Twelve and Twelve); and *Each Day a New Beginning,* a daily meditation book published by Hazelden. Jennifer says that at one point, she had been reading up to four meditation books but reports having cut back because "that was getting to be a bit much." Most of the women who talked to me say they read the ODAT every day. Judy says, "I've always kept the ODAT in my bathroom. When I get up in the morning, I do my insulin and my ODAT book. On the pot. Kill three birds with one stone. I figure once I read the book, I'm okay. I got in the habit of reading the book." In addition, Judy typically reads *Each Day* and a collection of daily meditations written for members of AA. Both Catherine and Jill read the ODAT and *Each Day* on a regular basis. Jill reports that she also reads the Big Book regularly, "not every day, maybe once a week probably." Tommie says that she doesn't read as much as she used to because she's "talking to more people" but says her daily reading includes "a few" meditation books.

When they discuss their reading, the women I interviewed use terms like escape, solace, solutions, identification, knowledge, acceptance, hope, growth, play, distraction, and "intense pleasure." They read as well, I believe, in order to "stimulate desire" and "extend the range of the possible," to borrow phrases from Barbara Sicherman (216). They read to create a self-aware life. They talk constantly about their reading, and this, in turn, contributes to a sense of community among them, though I admit it took me a while to see this.

In this chapter, I organize around what seem to be recursive, rather than linear, stages in the Mountain City women's reading. These stages appear more a deepening gyre than inevitable steps, though it seems that the first stage I describe below does in fact come first. As in the previous chapter, I use statements from the Al-Anon women to indicate different purposes and functions of their reading: "Identification was essential"; "The spoken word does help"; "an evolution in our reading"; "As you change, you can just see things differently"; "an intense pleasure"; "a communion of friendship."

Starting Recovery: "Identification was essential"

The women who talked with me read to identify the problem, and they read to identify with Al-Anon, which promises a solution to that problem. They read to understand the talk at the meetings and also to participate in the talk. But as they report, early on they were reading chiefly to find a name for the distress that had brought them to Al-Anon in the first place.

But when I asked the first thing they had read after coming to Al-Anon, both Tommie and Jill replied by talking about their reading *before* the program. Both Tommie and Jill, it seems, had used reading as a way to feel better: Tommie to make her life seem more "normal," Jill to find magical, though temporary solutions. Jill, in fact, speaks explicitly of her reading before Al-Anon as escape: "I used reading to escape, and it was a way that I did not have to deal. It was part of stuffing and denial. I still choose at some times to use it that way, and that's okay because I'm aware of it." This is not to say that the other women didn't or don't read for escape, but it is interesting that for both Tommie and Jill coming to program produced a contrast in their reading dramatic enough for each to remark upon it.

Before Al-Anon and during the time of her husband's heavy drinking, Jill read, she reports, "a lot of religious stuff," books "about healing and angels"; she says she also "read a lot about cults. I don't know why. I just did." Jill seems to have found solace in books that pictured supernatural solutions and intense community, themes that may indicate her feelings of helplessness and loneliness during the worst of her husband's drinking. Tommie's preprogram reading took a different tack: "For a period in my life—a few years ago, way before recovery—it was in my great lonely period—I read a lot of occult books, horror books. Things that just scared the shit out of you." In the intense emotions triggered by the occult books, Tommie apparently found relief from the problems of her daily life. In an essay called "Why We Crave Horror Movies," Stephen King claims that such stories help "re-establish our feelings of essential normality. . . . Freda Jackson as the horrible melting woman in 'Die, Monster, Die!' confirms for us that no matter how far we may be removed from the beauty of a Robert Redford or a Diana Ross, we are still light-years from true ugliness" (358). Compared to attacks by werewolves or vampires, the problems of living with an alcoholic fade, perhaps.

When I reiterated my question about the first thing she read after she came to Al-Anon, Tommie said,

> It wasn't a program book. It was *It Will Never Happen to Me* by Claudia Black. I was trying to read the Al-Anon litera-ture, but it was too overwhelming. I was looking for iden-tification. I couldn't identify with all of it—some of it, but not all of it. It was so foreign, and I think it was because of the language.

The language of Twelve-Step groups is obvious to outsiders, who often label it as jargon or make it the target of jokes and parody. Such terms as *surrender* or *turn it over, higher power, make amends, let go with love, one day at a time,* and *hit bottom* are all program terms, with more complex definitions and explanations than outsiders may realize. Specialized program language signals deep layers of meaning for the AA and Al-Anon communities, just as the specialized language of, say, composition studies has layers of meaning for readers of *CCC* or *JAC*. In using this language, program members "promote social cohesion by acting rhetorically upon themselves and one another," as Kenneth Burke explains in *A Rhetoric of Motives* (xiv). Indeed, according to Ernest Kurtz's history of AA, some of the program language in current use goes back to founders Bill W. and Dr. Bob. Moreover, the language of AA and Al-Anon directs members to a particular way of seeing, providing what Burke calls "a terministic screen." In *Language as Symbolic Action*," Burke explains that a given terminology—a terministic screen—both "direct[s] the attention" and establishes a lens through which to see—and interpret—the world (45).

Newcomers to Al-Anon often have difficulty with program language, which simultaneously includes and excludes, offering desired knowledge but in terms that seem strange, reminding the novice of her or his newcomer status. To be in the group, one has to understand the terms, and in order to claim membership, one has to use the terms appropriately. As a person begins to identify with the group, to recognize other members' experiences as similar to his or her own, the newcomer begins to use the group's terms for that experience. This is how identification works, how a person becomes "'substantially one' with a person [or group] other than himself" while "remain[ing] unique, an individual locus of motives" (Burke, *Rhetoric* 21). As Burke reminds us, if people were not already divided, there would be no need for identification, a rhetorical process that brings people together. Having been myself a newcomer to Al-Anon, I understand Tommie's problem with the unfamiliar program language. It was clear to me in my first meeting that I was observing the workings of a discourse community I did not know.

Critiquing the use of the concept of discourse community, Joseph Harris points out that compositionists have sometimes talked of the acquisition of unfamiliar discourse as "a kind of mystical leap of mind" that allows for stepping "cleanly and wholly" from one community to another. Instead, we should expect, Harris says, "a kind of useful dissonance as students are confronted with ways of talking about the world with which they are not wholly familiar" (17), explaining not just first-year college students' problems with academic literacy but also Tommie's early difficulty with the language of Al-Anon. The dissonance occurs not just on a vocabulary level but also on an interpretive or conceptual level, as Judy also makes clear in two stories about her early reading of program literature.

The first program piece Judy read was chapter 8 of the AA Big Book, "To the Wives":

> When my husband came home from treatment, the first thing he did was show me the Big Book of Alcoholics Anonymous. He said, "Chapter 8 is to the wives. Why don't you read that?" This was before I ever went to my first meeting, so I was walking around on eggshells. I don't care what the problem was [I'd say,] "It's okay." He thought I was nuts. I had a lot of anger, and I was saying, "Everything's fine." We'd meet in the hall, and I'd say, "Everything's fine." I read chapter 8, "To the Wives." This was nine years ago, remember. The only thing I got out of it was, Don't piss him off, he'll get drunk. That's not what it says at all. But that's all I could get out of it at the time.

A few weeks later, Judy went to her first Al-Anon meeting, where, she reports, she heard for the first time that she had not been the cause of her husband's drinking and where she saw that others with similar histories had achieved a life they perceived as better. At this meeting, she realized the importance of the ODAT book, even though she lacked the insider knowledge needed to read it:

> Everybody had one of them blue books. I kept saying, "Where can I get this book you people are reading out of? I have to have this." She [the chair of the meeting] said, "I forgot to bring them, they are at my house." "Give me your

address." I went to her house the next day, gave her the money, got my ODAT book, brought it home, and read it from front to back. Didn't understand a damn word of it. But I was just hungering for it. I knew that book had to be important because everybody else had one.

Her desire to "extend the range of the possible" in her life—what she metaphorically describes as a hunger for the secret of the other women's serenity—was Judy's motivation for reading. She knew, because everyone had one, that the book the Al-Anon women had was important, and she wanted what they had. In one meeting, she had begun to identify with the Al-Anon women and to realize the centrality of the ODAT book for how they identified themselves. But this is not the only identification for which the Mountain City women read.

In addition to Al-Anon literature, books on alcoholism or the affects of alcoholism on families are described explicitly by both Tommie, as we have already seen, and Lilly as "reading for identification." Lilly refers to books published by AA and Al-Anon as "program books" and nonprogram books that she and others read during this early phase as "recovery books," by which label she means books written by therapists or counselors about the family problems caused by various addictions. Among these recovery books were Sharon Wegscheder's *Another Chance* and Claudia Black's *It Will Never Happen to Me*. Both books, Lilly says, focus on adult children of alcoholics, and both recommend finding a support group as part of the recovery process. Lilly explains:

> We passed these around, especially *It Will Never Happen to Me*. We even named the Sunday night meeting after it, It Did Happen to Me. So it was very important. In the beginning, identification was essential. I needed to find someone who felt like I felt, who'd had an experience like I'd had. After a while that ceased to be so important. Claudia Black brought identification so close to all of us that it was like, Yes, that's what it is. Now we know that's what it is.

The other women who talked with me agreed that recovery books explained their own life experiences, offering concepts and labels they found useful, but all of them talked of reading such books early on and not going back to them again and again, as they do with Al-Anon literature. For example, Judy says,

> I have read co-dependency books. I've got *Co-Dependent No More* and the sequel to it and the Black, something by her. But I will honestly say I only read them once and I didn't reread them. If I like something, I'll reread it. There's something about those—I don't know whether it's conscience maybe because these weren't conference approved —I don't know what it was. I'm not saying I didn't get anything out of them. I probably did. But I didn't reread them, and that's strange for me.

Lilly explains why recovery books are not part of the ongoing reading of the Mountain City women:

> That's all they did was identify. Once you'd identified, so what? I didn't need anybody else to tell me what it was. I needed somebody to share with me how it could change. In the beginning of recovery, we shared recovery books and talked incessantly about those. And then I got to the place where I couldn't read them any more. I felt like this probably wasn't different for me, that this would happen with other people. Some people could never read recovery books very long at all.

For the Al-Anon women who talked to me, then, reading for identification seems to be an essential step. Identification is a key term and crucial concept, according to Burke in *A Rhetoric of Motives;* it is, he says, "an accessory to the standard lore" of persuasion (xiv). Identification, Burke explains, "ranges from the politician who, addressing an audience of farmers, says, 'I was a farm boy myself,' through the mysteries of social status, to the mystic's devout

identification with the source of all being" (*Rhetoric* xiv). Not associated with winning in the classical sense of argument, identification is the process by which people are brought together to form
social groups. The texts Lilly and Tommie call recovery books and
Judy calls co-dependency books set this sort of identification in mo-
tion: Early on, the women identify with the various roles the experts describe in their analyses of families of alcoholics. But these
books do not suffice for my research participants past this initial
stage. These recovery books seem to provide explanations that the
women read—to use Rosenblatt's term—"efferently," taking information from these texts. But these books apparently do not provide
an "aesthetic" reading experience the women wish to continue. As
we will see again, the Mountain City women prefer, when possible,
to read aesthetically, rather than efferently.

Through program literature, the Mountain City women then
begin, instead, to identify with—to become, in Burke's terms, "substantially one" with—the role Al-Anon delineates for them, that
of spiritual seeker. Al-Anon's message asks members to see themselves as moral and spiritual agents, a perspective that takes into
account a fuller humanity for women than the traditional view of
wife as helpmeet or dependent whose life someone else controls.
The recovery books seem to offer what Cornel West says are "indis-
pensable" analyses, but not the "affirmation of one's worth" essential to "the politics of conversion" (18–19) he posits as antidote to
the depression and hopelessness that structural powerlessness in-
flicts on members of oppressed groups.

This explanation is complicated, however, by sociologist Wendy
Simonds's findings of women reading self-help books. In her 1992
Women and Self-Help Culture: Reading Between the Lines, Simonds
reports that her research participants continue to read self-help
books even when they don't expect new information. The women
who talked to me differ in that they stopped reading the recovery or
co-dependency books from commercial publishers, but they are like
Simonds's participants in they have continued reading Al-Anon and
AA literature. A possible reason for discontinuing reading the recov-

ery books may be that the recovery books are not, as Judy mentioned, conference approved. Another reason may be that the participants in my study intuit what Simonds claims explicitly: that self-help books are "ideologically powerful instruments of cultural commerce that are linked both with the proliferation of buyable therapy, in which assistance comes to be seen as a purchasable commodity, and with the increasing volume of the marketplace for leisure consumption" (7). While many people in AA and Al-Anon have undergone therapy and a sizable minority are themselves professional counselors, a distrust of psychotherapy exists within the program community. It is not unusual in meetings to hear testimonies to the efficacy of the "working the program" over engaging expensive psychological counseling. The women who talked with me, I would argue, consider their program reading as part of a spiritual discipline—"equipment for living," in Burke's terms—and not as "buyable therapy."

The women who talked to Simonds "were unanimous in their recognition that self-help books were repetitive and thus secure. Reading could be a ritual of self-reassurance where repetition was *desired*" (26, Simonds's emphasis). It is certainly possible that the same motive applies in the case of the Mountain City women's repeated reading of program literature, but it is possible that another explanation exists as well. The popularity of self-help books derives from the "easy consolation" they offer, to use Burke's words ("Literature" 298). Burke asserts that few people attempt to apply the advice of "success" books because doing so would be difficult, requiring real changes (299). According to Burke, it is in the *act* of reading itself that readers attain symbolically what these books offer ("Literature" 299). Symbolic attainment seems to suffice for many readers.

The Mountain City women, however, seem to reach a place where they are no longer reading for identification of the problem, for easy consolation, or for symbolic solutions. They are reading, instead, for spiritual—emotional, psychological—growth, for the very change Burke says most readers eschew. When the Mountain

City women desire assurance, they go back, not to books that define the problem, offer buyable therapy, or provide symbolic achievement but rather to those that offer spiritual direction. They read now to identify with Al-Anon and with the Al-Anon group. They return, I argue, to books that can be read aesthetically, because these texts offer an experience of hope, provide different but possible roles for the women, and augment a sense of community among them. According to Simonds, "Reading can also—as I found with readers of religious books and feminist books—be used as a way of continually bolstering a reader's desired conception of the world" (32). My research participants' conception of the world is bolstered not by therapeutic recovery literature but by program reading, wherein their identities as members of a community are affirmed.

Reading AA Literature: "The spoken word does help"

For the Mountain City Al-Anon women, program reading includes AA material. From their comments about reading AA books, two issues emerge. The first has to do with Al-Anon policies on conference-approved literature (CAL). The second, the more important, is the relation between reading and talk.

The first issue is one we have seen already, in Judy's remark that perhaps one reason she had not reread the recovery books was that they were not conference approved. Conference-approved literature (CAL) is not just approved by Al-Anon; it is actually written and published by Al-Anon. The policy of using only CAL in meetings aims to keep Al-Anon from becoming identified with political or religious doctrines or with particular treatments or therapies that might dilute Al-Anon teachings, disrupt the harmony of a group, or turn people away. According to a recent Al-Anon magazine article, "[T]here is no limitation to what an individual may want to use for their recovery outside of the meetings, but . . . the Conference in 1969 clearly recommended the use of only CAL in meetings" ("Inside Al-Anon" 20). AA publications are not conference approved and therefore cannot be used in Al-Anon meetings. Some Al-Anon purists insist that because AA literature is for alcoholics, it is inappropriate for Al-Anon members even outside of meetings, but this hardline approach is not shared by my research participants, who all read AA material, often on a daily basis, as we have seen.

Of the women who participated in this study, Judy is the most explicit in her statements about this issue:

> I also have a great desire—and this doesn't go with Al-Anon, but I really don't give a damn—to know what's in AA books, too. Recovery is recovery to me. I think it's real important to read the phrase, to know the phrase, that they say in every AA meeting, in chapter 5 of the Big Book: There are some that are incapable of becoming sober. I think it's real important for any Al-Anon doing Twelfth-Step work to know that phrase: that it's possible—for someone they sponsor, for someone at a meeting—that her husband—may never get sober. He may die of it or go crazy. Don't ever give up hope. But also let them know that there are some out there who never get the program. That goes against World Service or conference-approved literature, but I don't care. People I sponsor get a copy of the Big Book. How else are you going to understand the disease?

Most of my research participants had high praise as well for AA's *Twelve Steps and Twelve Traditions.* Comparing the AA version to Al-Anon's *Twelve Steps and Twelve Traditions,* Jennifer responded by saying, "The AA Twelve and Twelve is more helpful . . . It seems to be written at a higher level, both reading and spiritual." Tommie, Catherine, and Judy all offered a similar opinion of the AA Twelve and Twelve. According to Tommie, "It doesn't leave things out. It keeps it simple." As Catherine lists the program titles she has read, she comments:

> I love the AA Twelve and Twelve. That to me is just very straightforward and clear. I like things to be real specific. It doesn't pull any punches. I can relate to it. Even though it's

about alcoholism, I can put my own personal problems in that and get help, some insight.

On the AA and Al-Anon Twelve and Twelve volumes, Judy replies with characteristic bluntness:

I like the AA Twelve and Twelve better than the Al-Anon one. Because they keep it simple. More simple than Al-Anon. AA calls a spade a fucking shovel. Al-Anon calls it a curved little tin thing with a handle. They say the same thing, only AA keeps it simple.

Throughout discussion of their program reading, the women speak favorably of publications like the AA Twelve and Twelve and Al-Anon's *Alateen: A Day at a Time,* which they describe as "simple." Although Judy is clear about what she means by "simple," what the others mean by this word is not. Certainly, the language of the Alateen book is easier than that of other program material because it is written for adolescents: the analogies are unsophisticated, and the vocabulary is familiar. So perhaps simple means accessible. The AA Twelve and Twelve was written, not for adolescents, but for adults whose drinking had damaged their own lives and those of their families and friends. Perhaps simple here means well written or persuasive. It is reasonable to assume that years of practice articulating the AA experience gave Bill W., the single author of the AA Twelve and Twelve, a particular eloquence, and perhaps years of dealing with alcoholics convinced him that straightforward language is more helpful than the circumlocutions or qualifications that lie at the heart of Judy's objections to the Al-Anon Twelve and Twelve. A text presenting an unequivocal and univocal solution laid out in clearly defined steps may seem simple to women whose lives have been anything but simple. The AA text may carry more cultural authority because Bill W. is seen as the authentic voice of AA or because he was a man. (Valuing texts because of the gender of the writer is not, after all, an unknown phenomenon.) Whatever the reason, the Mountain City women seem to find in this text not only the aesthetic experience they look for in their reading but also spiritual direction for the life they want to live—again, equipment for living.

Elaborating on her experience with the AA Twelve and Twelve, Catherine brings up the second issue emerging from the women's comments on their AA reading, the role of spoken language in learning how to read program materials:

> In Step Eleven, it talks about the St. Francis prayer. I've had a little bit of a problem with that prayer. I've seen some of it as meaning therefore you should not do any kind of hatred, you should only be nice. That's been a killer for me. I'm not sure that's the intention of the prayer, but in the past when I read it, it was like, you just don't do it. I've come to understand that to get to acceptance, you've got to do the feelings first. And I hadn't realized that. There again the spoken word does help. In order to get to forgiveness, you maybe do need to be real angry. Whereas in the church, it was just forgive.

The line in the St. Francis prayer (an indication of AA's connections with Christianity) that is problematic for Catherine is the one saying "where there is hatred, let me sow love." Catherine had taken this to mean that one simply should not hate, ever. Catherine's comment that "There again the spoken word does help" refers to the relation between reading and the oral tradition of the program, an issue that Catherine mentioned explicitly several times as she talked about her reading. According to Catherine, talk makes the meaning—the interpretation—of the texts clearer (as anyone who has ever been a member of a good graduate seminar knows). Eventually, the oral traditions of AA and Al-Anon find their way into print, of course, but it is the current talk that serves as context to Catherine's insight about the spiritual principles of the St. Francis prayer included in the AA Twelve and Twelve. In talk, in the oral tradition, Al-Anon members urge one another as they work Step Six and become "entirely ready" to ask "God to remove all these defects of character," not only to admit but also to experience (or re-experience) such negative emotions as anger and hatred. Male AA members may not need advice about admitting aggressive emotions, but many women in Al-Anon do. The spoken word instructs Catherine—and other women—to respond emotionally to the original injury before trying to reach forgiveness and humility. For Catherine, the AA text provides an explanation of spiritual ideals, but the Al-Anon oral teachings give her guidance on how to apply them.

The women who spoke with me reiterated again and again the necessity of talk. Looking at only what is printed in Al-Anon books and pamphlets and not at what is said in meetings and member-to-member yields an incomplete picture. The idea that a written text can be abstracted from its surroundings, from the lore that goes with it, from the oral tradition from which it comes, from other related texts, from the community it serves is common among those Charles A. Perfetti calls "hyperliterates." In other words, that a text stands alone is how some academics think or talk about reading (for example, Ong; Olson), but it is not how actual people read, if the women who talked to me can be said to be at all representative.

Concomitant with the Mountain City women's reading is, then, always the talk, the conversation, among them. Those scholars who see literacy and orality as dichotomous activities producing separate mental states and who share formalist assumptions about the nature of the text believe that "writing establishes what has been called 'context-free' language" (Ong 79) and thus argue that texts are "autonomous representations of meaning" (Olson 268). But for the Mountain City women, language, whether written or spoken, is never context-free, nor do they regard either the texts or their reading as autonomous. For them, reading depends on context—on the other texts one reads and on the talk one hears in meetings and member-to-member. For the Mountain City women who talked to me, there is no literacy without orality and no texts without contexts.

Tracking the Changes: "An evolution in our reading"

While the women I interviewed read a number of Al-Anon and AA publications, their main text is Al-Anon's *One Day at a Time,* the ODAT. For my research participants, reading the ODAT serves both as a path to change and as a way to track personal changes. When asked about what they read immediately after coming to Al-Anon, the women invariably mention the ODAT. Not only does Jen name the ODAT as the first thing she read after coming to Al-Anon, she can also cite the specific pages:

> There's an index in the back of the book. I read "Helping
> the Alcoholic" and probably "Alcoholism a Disease." Then
> I would read the page for the day, and that's about all I did.
> [Later] probably [the pamphlet] "Living with Sobriety"
> because my husband was in treatment.

Likewise, the ODAT was the first piece of Al-Anon literature for both Jill and Catherine, with Catherine mentioning, in addition, an Al-Anon pamphlet, "Alcoholism, a Merry-Go-Round Named De-nial," and an Al-Anon book, *The Dilemma of the Alcoholic Marriage.*

Reading the ODAT seems a necessary component of Al-Anon membership, at least for the Mountain City women. A book small enough (four by six inches) to fit easily in a purse, the ODAT was first published in 1973, a publication date indicating a world view formed even earlier. In the early days, Al-Anon membership con-sisted almost entirely of wives of AA members along with a few wives of still practicing alcoholics who were seeking some way to get their husbands sober and thereby save the marriage. The ODAT reflects this demographic and the attitudes toward marriage of those early members. In 1992, as a response to a changing mem-bership, Al-Anon published *Courage to Change: One Day at a Time in Al-Anon II,* also referred to as Daughter of ODAT by my research participants. The reason was "to more fully reflect the variety of our fellowship" (*Courage,* preface). By the late eighties, Al-Anon membership included husbands of female alcoholics, adult children of alcoholics, parents and siblings of alcoholics, people divorced from alcoholics, and partners of gay or lesbian alcoholics, in other words, people whose involvement with the alcoholic was not necessarily marriage or whose attitudes toward marriage might be more diverse than that of the earlier members.

But during the years that I was interviewing the Mountain City Al-Anon women, the original ODAT was still their chief Al-Anon text. The importance of this book for the Mountain City women was indicated by the elaborately hand-crocheted covers that many members had for their personal copies. Typically, these covers were gifts from other Al-Anon members, though some Mountain City women crocheted a variety of covers for their own books.

For many members, the ODAT is a compendium of the Al-Anon philosophy, which is summarized opposite the copyright page:

> This book suggests living One Day at a Time, and the ways in which we may find in each day a measure of comfort, serenity, and a sense of achievement.
>
> It discourages dwelling on past errors and disappointments; it visualizes the future only as a series of new days, each a fresh opportunity for self-realization and growth.
>
> Today is only a small manageable segment of time in which our difficulties need not overwhelm us. This lifts from our hearts and minds the heavy weight of both past and future.

The book itself is a collection of daily readings reflecting this philosophy. At the top of each page is the month, day, and page number. The body of each page contains a paragraph or two, sometimes three very brief ones, offering an anecdote or idea and a brief explanation. Near the bottom is "Today's Reminder," usually a six- to nine-line abstract of a lesson implied in the reading; this is followed by a quote from Scripture, from a philosopher or other well-known writer, or from an Al-Anon member (these are unsigned). An example:

TODAY'S REMINDER

I am not self-sufficient. I don't know all the answers. The answers I get, in fact, come to me as I keep myself receptive for them. Guidance comes from the group, from something I chance to read, and even from someone's word that providentially meets my need.

"God is our refuges and our strength,
a very present help in trouble."

Psalms

(ODAT 90)

At the back of the ODAT book is an index of subjects, among which are acceptance, alcoholism a disease, changing what I can, courage, detachment, divorce, expectations, fear, freedom, gratitude, humility, humor, joy, love, martyrdom, prayer, problem solving, self pity, and so forth. Following the index are the Twelve Steps, the Twelve Traditions, the Serenity Prayer, and the Slogans of Al-Anon. In publications of the ODAT since 1988, the Twelve Steps, Twelve Traditions, Slogans, and Serenity Prayer precede the index. Additionally, these editions include Al-Anon's Twelve Concepts of Service.

Meetings are often organized around a topic in the index. Various members read aloud the pages listed there. After the oral reading of each page, discussion or response follows, either by the person who read it or by someone else. The spoken responses often begin with phrases like "What this page reminds me of is the time when . . . " or "I first learned this when . . . " Then follows a brief personal anecdote on how the person had undergone a similar experience or had learned the lesson of the page under discussion. Sometimes, when a group has established that disagreements or questions are acceptable, someone will say, "I disagree with this because . . . " or "I don't understand how this works; it seems so foreign." The theme of the discussion is how the text applies to one's life.

"Read the literature" is a constant recommendation in Al-Anon meetings. Indeed the ODAT itself emphasizes the importance of reading:

> Right now I am reading something that will help me to grasp the Al-Anon philosophy. Right now I will set myself a program of reading the Al-Anon literature, which will help me to understand my problem and improve my outlook on life. Then I will be ready to solve my difficulties as they arise; then I will know when to stand aside and let them work themselves out. (23)

Reading is, then, a path for self-improvement for Al-Anon, an assumption about the uses of literacy shared by middle-class Protestants since the Renaissance (Scribner 77; Gere, "Common Properties" 384).

In addition to the ODAT page for the day, active members of Al-Anon read, either on their own or at the direction of a sponsor or some other program friend, the pages on topics appropriate for their particular problems. It is not uncommon for a participant in a meeting to say that she read all the pages on a particular topic—self-pity or anger, for example—as she dealt with some troubling situation. When people admit in meetings that they are struggling, veteran members typically respond by asking "Are you reading the literature?" or "Have you read the pages on [for example] detachment?" or by saying "When I feel like that, it helps me to read page eighty-six on acceptance" or "When that happened to me, I had to reread the pages on surrender." Faithful members know the ODAT intimately. As Jen put it, "I read the ODAT every day for five years. I can still pick out where the pages are."

With virtually constant discussion of the ODAT, the Al-Anon women differ from the women who talked to Simonds, who only rarely discussed their self-help reading: "Most women said that if it 'came up' in conversation, they would discuss their reading or that if they read a book that they thought was particularly applicable to a friend's life, they would recommend it" (43). The Mountain City women constantly put themselves in situations in which the topic comes up: meetings, conversations with sponsors, and social occasions with other members. ODAT reading is both a private and public activity. The actual decoding may take place individually, but the situations in which this reading takes place and the proper hermeneutics for understanding are delineated socially.

As the Al-Anon women change—their minds, their attitudes, their behavior—their reading changes. By noting how their reading, their interpretation, of the ODAT, has changed, the Mountain City women seemed to mark changes in themselves. The account of the most condensed and concrete changes comes from Judy, who explained how her reading of the ODAT changed during the first few weeks of her membership in Al-Anon. The day Judy got her copy, recall that she read it straight through, although she says now that she didn't "understand a damn word of it":

> Then I learned, after going to the second meeting, that I could be selective about what I read. I could look in the back for topics. I woke up and tried to figure out what I was—Was I happy? Was I sad?—so I would know what to read that day, still not realizing that you read the page for the date. About the third or fourth meeting, I finally saw the dates at the top of the page. It took me a month to start reading the page for the day.

According to Tommie, changes in what she pays attention to as she reads the ODAT signal either personal growth, the need for it, or both:

> You read the ODAT every day, and three years later you say, I never saw that in there before, and I know I've read that a hundred times. So it lets me know what I'm supposed

to think about. I think it's because we grow and change. When it jumps off the page, I feel it first, then my head will grasp it intellectually. There's an evolution in our reading. We get it when we're ready to receive it, ready to feel it.

Lilly explains that her reading of the ODAT has changed as well:

When I started reading it, to me it was a lot of Hallmark stuff, and I didn't like that at all. But then I didn't like anything in Al-Anon. It was all Hallmarky. Platitudes. Slogans. Very trite. But I was so lost and so desperate I was willing to do anything. And the meetings felt right. So when people suggested I do certain things, I just did them. And the ODAT was one of them. And it grew on me. I began to realize I could take what I liked and leave the rest. And, over time, there was a lot to take.

When Lilly says she realized she could "take what [she] liked and leave the rest," she is quoting from Al-Anon's closing ritual, wherein members are reminded that taking the program "whole," or all at once, is not required. This is one of those phrases, like "God as we understood Him" in the steps, that indicate tolerance for a range of individual views (see Kurtz on why this was important in the early days of AA).

Reading the ODAT is not always a smooth process for the other Mountain City women, either. As with Lilly, there is resistance along the way, though sometimes it is more the message and not the style that is the problem. Jill says that she doesn't disagree as much as she used to with the ODAT, but, she recalls: "I used to read, and I'd just go, 'Ha! This is not right!' Especially those ones about 'and two months later he got sober.' I have a little bit of forgiveness for that now. I can read those pages now that he's been sober six months." For Tommie, disagreeing with what she reads is still difficult: "That is still a courage issue for me. I'll ask someone else to read it. Then I'll talk with them about it. 'What did you think about so-and-so?'" Judy explains her disagreements:

I'm not saying that the things that are written down are wrong. I would do them differently. It says in the ODAT book, Don't yell at the alcoholic, this, that, and the other. I found in my own personal experience, sometimes you can't keep your mouth shut. You can say things, but you don't have to be angry about it or hostile or raging or yelling. But you can point things out: This is unacceptable behavior. It says in the ODAT book that you don't yell at the alcoholic or scream at him. I have learned to use that and turn it around to my advantage.

Judy is not the only one who has had difficulty with the "little woman" ideology that is incorporated into the ODAT. Lilly explains:

I went through a phase where it really began to irritate me again. The main focus seemed to me to be spouses and that you needed to do all these things so the whole house would be better or the relationship would be better or the marriage would be better, that there was less focus on you doing this so you would be better. The focus was on you doing this so all this other would be better. That was the thing that made me the craziest.

Now I realize that has to do with the language and the attitudes of the times, which is why they're rewriting it.

But I got so angry once I just threw it. It hit the wall in the kitchen, and I broke the back of my book. But I kept reading, because it was important when I started.

Lilly believes that such instances of reading against the text are common with people in the program:

There has been a whole segment of people who have gone through phases with the ODAT when they get real frustrated and angry or disappointed. Big feelings about it. It's happened in meetings. An oldtimer about a month ago at

Tuesday morning meeting—we read a page, and her comment was "I totally disagree with this page. This page tells
me I have the power to change myself." And there she
went. I thought, Yeah, that could be one of the implications of this page. And I remembered being that angry and
throwing the book. But there are also other implications on
that page. It doesn't have to be that black and white. It can
be where we are. So, yeah, I think it happens to everybody.

The anger exhibited in these two stories is, I would argue, a
form of Rosenblatt's aesthetic reading, despite our typical understanding of *aesthetic* as something pleasant. Rosenblatt means the
term in the sense of experiencing as we read, of reacting to the
reading with emotion, not a particular emotion. Strong emotion,
whether positive or negative, makes a text more memorable, more
powerful, and the experience of reading more vivid. Rosenblatt
would say that Lilly's anger has diminished because she herself has
changed: she has more information about the cultural and social mi-
lieu in which the ODAT was written; she has a generally positive
frame from her experience with the program to put this negative
message into. When the reader changes, the transaction between
the reader and the text—the meaning—changes.

*Locating Meaning: "As you change, you can just
see things differently"*

Neither anger nor resistance is the end of the process of reading the
ODAT for Lilly:

And it's changed again. Right now [the ODAT] has things
to say that I didn't realize were quite so spiritual when I
read them over the first nine years. They have gotten more
spiritual, and that probably has to do with me. It's always
been there. But as you change, you can just see things differently.

Given Lilly's remark about the changing meaning of the ODAT, I asked, "Was the spiritual message you are now finding always in the text, or are you now bringing it to the text?" Lilly answered, "I can't be absolutely sure. I do believe that something was always there. I don't know how much was there. So I don't know exactly what I bring to it in terms of adding to it, [but] I do."

Jennifer has a similar view of the relationship of texts, meaning, and readers. In one conversation in which we talked not about reading the ODAT but about reading other kinds of texts, Jennie explained that a text doesn't have to fit into a neat category called spiritual in order to be the source of a spiritual message:

> Anything I read I can find spirituality in it. Even a comic strip in the newspaper. If the person is writing a message, trying to make a specific point, and that paper goes to 20,000 people, not all 20,000 readers will get what the writer is saying, but for maybe 200 people, it might make an impact on them.

I asked, "So the spiritual message is not on the page, not in the text, but in the reader?" "Well," Jen replied, "in the writer and the reader. So in a sense it's in the text. But unless you know what it is—unless it's something you'd recognize and that's going to make a difference in your life—you probably won't pick up on it." Jennie believes that it is through reading with an awareness of the possibility of a spiritual message that she finds it

Jennie's explanation is remarkably similar to Stanley Fish's reading of the *Areopagitica*. In a 1987 essay "Driving from the Letter: Truth and Indeterminacy in Milton's *Areopagitica*," Fish states that in a number of earlier texts, Milton clearly disapproves of setting the letter—that is, books, even the Bible—above the spirit of the law. Fish points out that the praise of books in the *Areopagitica* does not square with Milton's theology and then sets out to show that in the *Areopagitica*, Milton does, indeed, maintain his theology. According to Fish, Milton first asserts that virtue (or meaning or, in the case of my research participants, a spiritual insight or message) resides not in a book, not in an object, but in ourselves (238). Milton immediately contradicts himself, saying that virtue (or meaning or spirituality) is not *in* us to start with, for as human beings we are not naturally pure but naturally sinful (Fish 241). The dilemma is bleak, Fish explains: "If purity can be found neither in books, where it first seemed to reside, nor in naturally pure hearts, where the argument next seemed to place it, then it cannot be found anywhere" (241). But Milton reassures us that virtue is attainable, reminding us that "that which purifies us is triall and triall is by what is contrary" (qtd. in Fish 241). In Fish's terms, "[purity] can only be made by sharpening it against the many whetstones provided by the world" (241). Acting as this whetstone, as "what is contrary" (240), books help us remove sin and thereby attain purity, or virtue, by supplying opportunities for us to exercise "the faculty of judgment" (242). The point is that virtue (or meaning or spirituality) is made, created, brought into being by our interactions with the text. It is through the exercise of reading for truth (or purity or meaning or spirituality) that we find it. Though we may not begin as pure, through reading we become pure. To paraphrase Fish, spirituality is heightened by sharpening it against the whetstone of texts. As Fish puts it, "The moral, then, is not 'seek and ye shall find,' but 'seek and ye shall become'" (246).

While Jennie, like Fish, seems to locate meaning in the interaction of reader and text or in the interaction of reader and writer by means of the text, Catherine appears to think that the spiritual message is located more in the reader than in the text. She explains her awareness that she reads from her own perspective:

> I was reading a mystery. Here's this line here and that one there—a message for me, kind of a message for my spiritual growth. And I basically don't like mysteries. But there it was, right there. I loved *Cold Sassy Tree*. For instance, the line in there I just hang on to was 'Faith means it's going to be all right.' The other line I love from *Cold Sassy Tree* is— and here is the Catholic connection—see how I find me or something I want?—the Grandfather is saying the miracle

is not the virgin birth but that this mother let her son be. To me, that is neat. Especially as a mother.

Here Catherine seems to be voicing Norman Holland's argument that

> readers respond to literature in terms of their own 'life style' (or 'character' or 'personality' or 'identity')"—that is, "an individual's characteristic way of dealing with the demands of outer and inner reality. . . . what the individual brings with him to any new experience, including the experience of literature. (5 *Readers Reading* 8)

It is this identity, Holland argues, that is the basis of literary interpretation: "[A]ll of us, as we read, use the literary work to symbolize and finally to replicate ourselves. We work out through the text our own characteristic patterns of desire and adaptation" ("Unity" 124). Holland and other literary critics, such as I. A. Richards and David Bleich, base their theorizing on responses from actual readers, typically college students, and they talk as if the patterns of response were unconscious. Indeed, it may be that for many readers that is so. Lack of self-awareness certainly seems not to be the case with Catherine, who appears quite conscious that her identity as a Catholic and as a mother influences her reading and that her identity as a spiritual seeker allows her to see spiritual messages even in texts like mysteries that she doesn't particularly like.

The Mountain City Al-Anon women are conscious that their reading of the ODAT changes over time, with Judy telling us that her reading of the ODAT changed significantly over a period of weeks and Lilly tracing the changes in her reading over nine years. The women who talked to me indicate that it is in the process of reading that they find the spiritual message they are looking for. They are aware that what they see in the text depends on what they bring to the reading. As Lilly puts it, she "adds" to the spiritual message of the ODAT. The spiritual insights my research participants seek in their reading are found in their interaction with the texts, sometimes in their struggles with "what is contrary" in the Al-Anon philosophy. They find spiritual messages in the texts they read because Al-Anon talk has provided a terministic screen, focusing these women to look for those messages and has given them language to describe their perceptions.

For the Mountain City women, interpretation is multiple; they know this from their own histories with the ODAT and from sharing interpretations with one another. They learn that reading is not merely an individual, private activity but also a function of the group. They learn that interpretation entails choice, as Lilly points out when she says that she learned that she could, as Al-Anon itself puts it, take from the ODAT what she liked and "leave the rest." For the Mountain City women, then, meaning is not a property of texts. For them, meaning changes over time and with readers. None of the Mountain City women who talked with me has ever heard of Stanley Fish or Norman Holland, nor have they engaged in any formal study of theories of reading or interpretation, nor do they typically spend time talking about the indeterminacy of the text or about the location of meaning. Nonetheless, these concepts appear to be illustrated in these women's accounts of their reading. For them, the theoretical wars that have tested the civility of English departments over the last decades would be surprising.

Letting Change Happen: "An intense pleasure"

Although the Mountain City Al-Anon women read in order to grow spiritually, at the same time they read for fun, recreation, and pleasure, for, as they put it, distraction and play. Here are the murder mysteries, true-crime stories, movie star biographies, science fiction novels, romances, and serious literary works like *Beloved* and *One Hundred Years of Solitude*—in other words, the genres many Americans read for entertainment. The purpose of this kind of reading, Lilly explains, is also aesthetic: it moves people away from "intense focus" on their own lives, problems, and efforts to change, offering a "lightness" and "ease" that stand in contrast to the heavy work of recovery from what Lilly calls the "dis-ease."

In some ways this reading sounds like the reading for escape described by Jill and Tommie, but two things distinguish this reading: purpose and content. First, the purpose of this reading seems to be neither avoiding or minimizing a problem nor looking for magical solutions, as it was for Jill and Tommie before they came to Al-Anon, with Jill's books about supernatural healing, angels, and cults and Tommie's horror stories that "would just scare the shit out of you." The reading the women do for pleasure does not seem intentionally aimed at avoiding problems but rather giving oneself a break from them. As I explain in this section, this reading is for recreation, in the almost literal sense of the word.

Second, unlike the material used for escape, the books the women read for pleasure, distraction, and play, although nonprogram, nonrecovery material, and chiefly fiction, do, in fact, as Tommie phrases it, "touch on the disease" as well as on other issues in the women's lives. References to these issues, even oblique ones, disallow pure escape. Jill, for example, reads books about people with multiple personalities, most of whom, she says, suffered sexual abuse. "I read to see that I'm okay," she says. Jill's reading is not limited to this subject, however, and includes other popular genres:

> I don't read fiction that isn't a murder mystery or science fiction, although I do once in a while read romances. David reads nothing but nonfiction. There are certain books that he brings home that really interest me. My sister buys a lot of books about mass murders, and I read those when she gets done with them. I don't purchase them, but I can read them.

Judy's reading for play centers mostly on biographies:

> I'm a biography buff. I love it. In fact every time I go to the store I pick up a new biography. Right now I'm reading about Diana Ross. My hobby is old movies, movie stars. I like the lives of the thirties' and forties' stars because they

were always screwing somebody they weren't supposed to.
I love to read that kind of trash.

Admitting to being "very nosy," Judy reports that she owns two
books about the private lives of the rich and famous, *Who Had Who*
and *Sex Lives of Famous People,* and that she particularly enjoys
People among the magazines she regularly reads. She likes a novel
once in a while, she says. In contrast to the recovery books that Judy
read only once, the books she likes she often re-reads: *Sex Lives of
Famous People* two or three times and *Gone with the Wind* seventeen
times.

Judy is very much aware that her movie star biographies "touch
on the disease":

> When I read my biographies and when I watch TV, I can
> pick out a program person. The other night I was watching
> TNN and Johnny Cash was on. He said, 'When I get these
> feelings'—I know he didn't think of what he was saying—'I
> call Waylon. He's recovering, too.' And I perked up. One
> thing I do, subconsciously I'm sure, is pick a person out, a
> recovering person, if I'm reading about them in an article.
> I think that's one reason I avidly read biographies nowadays.
> Because, especially the movie stars back in the thirties and
> forties, the booze flowed like you wouldn't believe. You can
> see who had a problem with booze.

When Tommie talks about the reading she does for fun, she
mentions specifically Shirley MacLaine's autobiographies and science fiction novels. But her comments on the changes in her reading
demonstrate that reading for distraction and for fun is intentional
and conscious, qualities that further help distinguish this reading
from her earlier escape reading:

> I got out of reading for a long time. When I met Lilly, read-
> ing came back into my life. I'd got so involved in learning,
> I was reading all this stuff about adult children. And she

realized something—she said, "You've got to stop reading. You need to change your focus. Because you are disappearing into the words." She started giving me the Spenser books. So I started reading mystery detective books. They were wonderful stories. They sort of touch on the disease, but there's a bigger focus. I loved the Spenser books.

Tommie is talking here about Robert B. Parker's series of detective novels. The protagonist is ex–prize fighter Spenser. The other characters include Susan, the psychologist girlfriend, and Hawk, the African American tough guy and friend. Tommie is also referring to the two kinds of reading Rosenblatt describes. When Tommie says, "I got so involved in learning, I was reading all this stuff about adult children," she means that she was reading to learn, to acquire information. This is the reading Tommie has categorized as reading for identification, specifically texts offering descriptions of the behavior of children and spouses of alcoholics. It is Rosenblatt's efferent reading, that is to say, reading "in which the primary concern of the reader is with what he will carry away from the reading" (24). When Tommie explains that she had "got out of reading for a long time," she means she had not been reading for pleasure or for the experience of the reading, what Rosenblatt calls aesthetic reading. In this kind of reading, "the reader's primary concern is with what happens *during* the actual reading event. . . . *In aesthetic reading, the reader's attention is centered directly on what he is living through during his relationship with that particular text*" (24–25, Rosenblatt's emphasis).

Tommie's recovery of aesthetic reading—"They were wonderful stories. . . . I loved the Spenser books"—began with the Spenser mysteries that Lilly had given her. Lilly had lent the Parker detective novels to others among the Al-Anon women. Both Jennie and Catherine report reading the Spenser books. The mystery that seemed to Catherine to have spiritual messages just for her was, in fact, one of the Spenser novels. In explaining her reason for lending these books, Lilly argues persuasively for the importance of recreational, or aesthetic, reading:

You can work too hard at something. I can focus so intently on change, to grow and work so hard that I get stuck in the work and there is no change. I believe greatly in distraction, in play, because when I came to recovery, finding this woman in Memphis who played changed how I felt about so many things. Although I didn't think anything was changing, at least we'd gone to the park and we'd laughed. We'd taken the kids and we'd spent time with them.

It's hard work. Even in theater, it's ninety-nine percent sweat, one percent talent. So work was it. I knew about work. I didn't understand the importance of play and laughter. I began to understand what theater does, that it really adds to one's being able to grow and change because there is a distraction of beauty, laughter, and joy that allows you to participate in the change without needing to have power over it.

That's been important with certain people in recovery who are as intense as I am—to participate in the distraction. We'll get together, we'll have slumber parties and be silly and do whatever, we'll go to movies, we'll laugh. And books have been a great part of that.

I've realized that reading is an intense pleasure. You can learn from it. It can be painful. It can be all kinds of things. But I always thought reading had to do with school and learning. It was not a fun thing. It was not a soothing thing. That, in recovery, has just blossomed.

I was very impatient when I came to recovery. Having children helped that a little, slowed me down a little. Spiritual growth is difficult if you aren't patient. There's a lot of waiting. That's why the distraction is so important. You need to be busy, not just your physical being, but your emotional and spiritual being so that things can work in your life. You can only do so much work, then you have to live so the rest of it can take shape.

This explanation was not the response I had expected. As an academic all my life, I have learned so thoroughly to read efferently —that is, for information—that I had been quite sure the content of Parker's detective fiction was Lilly's main consideration. I had expected Lilly to say that she gave the Spenser books to her Al-Anon friends because Parker's characters are typically people with broken places and because Spenser, the hero, attempts to protect these people or to protect others from the damage they do out of their woundedness. While Lilly did not disagree about the content of the books--this was after all how they "touched on the disease," one of the things that distinguishes this kind reading from pure escapism —she did deny that the content was her main reason for sharing them. It was, rather, the experience of reading these books, the distraction they offered from the intensity of recovery work; these books, according to Lilly, lent themselves to aesthetic reading, while touching on the disease but not focusing exclusively on it.

Elaborating, Lilly said that the Spenser books provide a "lightness of reading," by which term I assumed she meant merely a fairly easy reading level—that is, not intellectually or linguistically difficult. This turns out, however, not to be what Lilly is talking about when she talks about reading being valuable because it is "light." When I asked Lilly for more explanation, she spent some time explicating the concept of "lightness," though somewhat indirectly:

> I really like the relationship between Spenser and Susan in terms of the connections because they were so different from each other, from such different backgrounds, but they blended, how they gave to the relationship and how honest they were. It also is wonderful reading because he gets into how the characters trust and care about each other— like with Hawk—the implicit trust. Yet Hawk is a person that neither Spenser or Susan would ever want to have on the other side because of his amoral belief system. I like that character in terms of how different he was, and yet what was important to him was a lot of qualities that

are important to most people. It was good reading. When we've talked about those mysteries, we talk a lot about the relationships.

For Lilly, then, "light" entails stories where the central characters deal with one another calmly, honestly, unambiguously, humorously, and respectfully, across lines of class and race. These characters offer models for relationships unfamiliar to many people in Al-Anon, whose own relationships have been fraught with anger, hurt, deceit, or confusion. What these books provide is not analysis but the possibility of relationships that can be "light."

In addition, Lilly also means, as I have come to see, light as opposed to dark in a spiritual sense. She says, by way of further illustration, that Elmore Leonard's books are "too dark" for some people:

> If you want diversion, reading Elmore Leonard takes you into the depths of something that might be a little too painful. Also, in a world that some of us have touched into, the emotional violence is so much more intense and not as complete in the circles it makes. Spenser always completes everything. They're happy-ending books. Leonard's books aren't. There's resolution, but a lot stays hanging.

That Lilly's phrase "the lightness of reading" has a spiritual connotation becomes clearer as she turns to Tony Hillerman's mystery novels:

> Hillerman has even more of a spiritual light because he does the Native Americans, the Navajo, and so he has a lot of threads in terms of how that spiritual life works in terms of living and resolving the mysteries of life as well as the mystery he's trying to solve. The young police officer who is trying to be a spiritual leader, a medicine man, he's doing ritual throughout the books and gets more and more adept at it. So those are quite interesting. They make a great

conversation about what ritual does and what you learn
from oldtimers, what gets passed down from generation to
generation that's important in terms of the cycle of life.
And that's also very light reading.

The lightness of reading that Lilly describes in terms of characters and themes may also be part of the reader's attitude, as Catherine indicates. In the interviews, Catherine referred several times to
her difficulties with reading: that she didn't see herself as much of a
reader, that she felt that she didn't retain facts, that she didn't get
the big picture. These comments didn't jibe with what I knew of
Catherine's reading; certainly by English department standards she
read good novels, Toni Morrison's *Beloved* and Gabriel Garcia Mar-
quez's *One Hundred Years of Solitude,* for example. Presented with
this discrepancy, Catherine elaborated: "I think historically I've
read everything as if it is true. I think I thought that if it's printed,
it's true." As a result, Catherine has been, she says, troubled by, put
off by, or rejecting of materials that deviated from what she has been
taught or has believed to be right. Catherine had not therefore
found reading a relaxing—or "light"—activity. As a young woman,
Catherine, a Catholic, had been "very much caught up in the Le-
gion of Decency." Her need to follow the rules of the Church has
influenced her reading, but that need has changed as she herself has
changed, allowing her to "participate in the distraction" of reading:

Through the years, I've gotten very nervous in books with
sexually explicit scenes. It's occurred to me that I've missed
a lot of other stuff that was going on because I got so
uptight about this. Two years ago my daughter, who was
twenty-one and home for the holidays, said, "Mom, I'd
like you to go to the movies with me, to see 'Rain Man.'"
She very calmly said, "Mom, it's R-rated." The way she
said it, there was an acceptance. This is right after I've realized that I'd been so caught up with some scenes that
I've missed other messages. So I went to this movie. I en-
joyed being with her presence. I was impressed with her

perceptions. I thought it was excellent. I really couldn't see
why it was R-rated.

After this incident, Catherine says that reading became "easier" for
her. It seems that awareness of having missed important things and
the company of her daughter allowed Catherine to experience this
film aesthetically, and that once she had knowledge of that kind of
"reading," she able to carry that ability over to printed material,
as well.

The Mountain City women serve as a reminder that distraction,
play, and pleasure are important motives for reading. Lilly explains
that this kind of reading permits people to "participate in the distraction" that allows psychological changes to occur. In an age in
which art often offers images of darkness and meaninglessness,
Lilly argues that "beauty, laughter, and joy" are essential. For Lilly,
this reading is not just entertainment, but re-creation, in the etymo-
logical sense of the word. She puts it in the same category with
slumber parties and movies, offering us a reminder that we read not
just for the meaning but also for the experience, something often
neglected in school, where efferent reading is privileged over aesthetic reading.

This is a point Anne Gere makes in her 1994 article "Common Properties of Pleasure: Texts in Nineteenth-Century Women's
Clubs." Examining reading in women's clubs in the nineteenth century, Gere says that the literate practices of the clubwomen often ran
counter to the school tradition of reading only for information:
"[T]he study of literature in schools and colleges allowed little room
for affective responses and multiple interpretations" (388). Gere
says that by "valuing pleasure over economic profit and emphasizing aesthetics over functional concerns," the clubwomen readers
subverted the dominant ideology of schooling (397).

Similarly, in a case study of women's reading in late-Victorian
America, Sicherman cites one family's comments about a female
relative who "'lost herself' in books" and "loved reading passion-
ately" (203), just as a hundred years later, Tommie says she "loved
the Spenser books." For the women in the family Sicherman studied,

reading was the "intense pleasure" that Lilly describes. Sicherman argues that the reading of these women was "not simply a passive form of cultural consumption"; instead, she asserts that for them reading "stimulates desire rather than simply pacifying it" and "extends the range of the possible" (216). Stimulating desire and extending the range of the possible are, I believe, what Lilly means when she uses the relationships of the characters in the Spenser novels to explain to me what she means by "the lightness of the reading." But stimulating desire and extending the range of the possible are the functions of other texts as well. Judy has told us that she has "a great desire to know what's in the AA books" because "recovery is recovery to me." Jennifer and Catherine attest to finding spiritual messages in comic strips and novels. For the Mountain City women, many kinds of books function to stimulate desire and extend the range of the possible.

Despite academic studies that discuss reading in terms of grade level or speed, both Gere and Sicherman use language that points to another area of human life—pleasure, love, passion, and desire—terms similar to or the same as those used by the Mountain City women to describe their aesthetic reading—joy, pleasure, love, play. These are not terms traditionally used in mainstream Anglo-American literary criticism. French critic Roland Barthes, however, takes seriously the "pleasure of the text," arguing for its recognition in his book of that title. Here Barthes distinguishes between what his translator calls texts of pleasure and texts of bliss, asserting that texts of pleasure bring comfort while texts of bliss are associated with a more explicitly sexual response. Although the usefulness of this distinction is not altogether clear, what is crucial to a fuller understanding of literacy, I believe, is Barthes's insistence that responses to texts are located not only in the intellect but in the body as well. In "A Note on the Text" in Barthes's *The Pleasure of the Text,* Richard Howard says that Barthes's contribution to criticism is "an erotics of reading" (viii). But Barthes knows that his view of literary experience is unusual: "No sooner has a word been said, somewhere, about the pleasure of the text, than two policemen are ready to jump on you: the political policeman and the psychoanalytical policeman: futility and/or guilt, pleasure is either idle or vain, a class notion or an illusion" (57).

In trying to write about something that he claims is beyond words, Barthes says that texts of bliss depend on indirection, giving hints or flashes, disrupting easy cultural assumptions. These texts invite reading that is not at a steady pace but rather reading varying in intensity and speed, Barthes says, clearly pointing to an erotic response. Such an explanation is, interestingly, similar to Janice Radway's explication of the reading of romance novels by her research participants—both erotic in that certain scenes could be classed as soft porn and disruptive in that they point, for her readers, to a different politics of sexuality, one in which the woman's sexual pleasure is the goal of the encounter.

Arguing for the value of texts of bliss, Barthes says this kind of reading fosters creativity:

> To be with the one I love and to think of something else: this is how I have my best ideas, how I best invent what is necessary to my work. Likewise for the text: it produces, in me, the best pleasure if it manages to make itself heard indirectly; if, reading it, I am led to look up often, to listen to something else. (24)

This seems to me to be another way of saying what Lilly has explained: that reading for pleasure or for play invites one's emotional, psychological, and spiritual work to come to fruition while one is otherwise distracted. The watched pot never boils.

The pleasure of the text is associated, for Gere, with the pleasure the clubwomen took in the multiple interpretations of texts generated by their discussions. In these affective responses, or aesthetic readings, the women joined together, Gere argues, not only to resist a "book-dominated view of discourse"—that is to say, one in which the book is privileged over the readers—but also to establish "an alternative erotics of learning" ("Common Properties" 390), a view that recalls the change in Lilly's reading: "I always thought reading had to do with school and learning. It was not a fun thing. It was not a soothing thing. That, in recovery, has just blossomed." For Lilly, reading is now an "intense pleasure." Unlike the traditional male erotics of learning, the female version seems, as we see in the next section, less individual and more communal.

Sharing Responses: "A communion of friendship"

At the center of the Mountain City women's reading is Lilly. Jennifer, Tommie, and Catherine all report that Lilly had lent them the Spenser mysteries, other novels, and the De Mello meditation books. Both Tommie and Jennie talked about not being able to afford to buy reading material and of borrowing magazines and books from others, specifically from Lilly. The women didn't always refer to Lilly by name; sometimes they referred to her as "my sponsor." Catherine, for instance, talked of "my sponsor" lending books to her, recommending specific titles, and advising her to finish *The Color Purple* when Catherine found the early pages troubling.

In Mountain City, Al-Anon members do not name their sponsors publicly; this information is considered part of the anonymity required by the program. Therefore during the early interviews, I did not ask the women who talked to me who their sponsors were because I knew this question would make them uncomfortable and also because at the time I didn't think the identity of their sponsors mattered. But having attended meetings in Mountain City myself, I was aware that Lilly sponsored a number of Al-Anon members, and as I listened to the women, it became clear that Lilly sponsored Jennifer, Catherine, and Tommie. Surmising that Jill's sponsor was Jennifer, I asked explicitly, and Jill replied affirmatively. Lilly and Judy had become friends early on because they had been in the program for about the same length of time and had often worked together in the Al-Anon organization. Later, when I did ask, all these relationships were confirmed. As these connections emerged, I began to see what I had previously thought was a loose network of acquaintances was actually a tightly knit community of friends, with Lilly as an important member. Two years after the first set of interviews, I talked with Lilly. When I explained that I wanted to interview her because I now saw these women as a community that included her, her response was "Oh, I like that. Yes, that's how I see it, too."

When asked why she recommended certain books to certain people, Lilly replied, "I'll give someone a book because it says something that I haven't got the words for, haven't got my mind around enough to share. Sometimes they won't get exactly what I'm trying to say, but they give me back something I missed." One book that Lilly has lent that falls into this category is Joyce Carol Oates's *Son of the Morning,* the story of Pentecostal preacher who finally collapses under the expectations of his congregation. Lilly explains why she lends this book:

> A lot of people come to recovery with intense Bible-belt religion. But intense religion gets in the way of spiritual growth because of all the rules that you learn of what is acceptable and what isn't. There's certain elements of spiritual growth we're very frightened of. If people are really into the rules, they get very nervous about moving into other spiritual avenues, because that's diluting their religion, or it might even be the devil's workshop. *Son of the Morning* really touched a lot of that. It's an incredible book, but it's hard to read.

Sometimes in her role as sponsor, Lilly is more directive and intuitive, as she illustrates recounting this incident:

> I said to someone once, I'd like for you to read everything you can on self-righteousness. She was so furious. That was not anything I'd planned [to say]. It just came to me. Her reaction was intense, so I knew I was right. It was not clear to me why I did that. I realized I didn't have any control over that. I had to trust what came. She didn't come back for three days, and when she did, she understood why I did it. It was real exciting but a little scary.

Lilly's influence on the reading of the other women is not always directly tied to their personal growth but rather to her own needs and experience. Lending books to others is an intentional act, part of the way she lives her life:

> I went to a woman's college. So I've grown up in communities of women. I came up with a philosophy, since I came from a poor family and a lot of my friends didn't have much, either. It was what I called Whoever Has, Pays. When I moved to New York with a friend, that was our philosophy. So coming into recovery felt very good in the sense that I like that community feeling. I still believe Whoever Has, Pays, to a point.

Lilly explains, without giving any details, that she has amended this philosophy somewhat: "I can be too generous, and that can hurt me and anybody I'm giving to. I've learned a lot about giving too much." Lending books is different: "If I have a book that somebody doesn't have, they can always borrow it. I like the discussions with the people after we've read the books. You can't have the discussion unless you're willing to share the books." Unless the book is a recovery book or Al-Anon literature, it is her own need, Lilly says, more than the other person's that brings her to share a book.

Sometimes the book Lilly lends is not her idea, but someone else's:

> Often Tommie will find something. Tommie doesn't have the money to buy them. So if she talks about a book, I'll buy it, and we'll start it around. Or she might even start it, start reading it first. Then I'll end up with the book at the end, because I've bought it. It will make a circuit. I've discovered I can trust Tommie's choices. It will always be an incredible conversation. Whether it's a book I want to keep in the end, I don't know. That doesn't seem to matter.

Physically sharing books is common to women's groups, as Gere reports in the "Common Properties" article. It was not an unusual practice, she reports, for a woman's club to buy one copy of a title and either read it aloud in the group or, like the Mountain City Al-Anon women, pass it around among the members (387–88). In addition, according to Gere, "members shared their personal libraries . . . as they gathered material for writing" (391). The reasons for sharing may range from women's traditional poverty to lack of control of finances to an ingrained reluctance to buy for themselves. Whatever the reason, these reading practices undermine the capitalistic concept of the book as commodity, Gere argues. But perhaps even more important, as Gere shows and as my research participants affirm, sharing the actual text leads to sharing interpretations of the text, both practices nurturing the sense of community among the women.

The sharing—the talk, the oral conversation that follows a book as it is passed around the circle—is arguably the most significant aspect of the reading of the Mountain City women. It may be more accurate to say, though, that the discussions of books are embedded in ongoing conversations of the Al-Anon women. In this talk, more than in the reading itself, the Mountain City Al-Anon women "come to voice," for it is in these conversations that the women explore, translate, clarify, and articulate their feelings and beliefs on any number of issues. According to Lilly, books that effect an emotional response—that is, those that "trigger feelings"— become the catalyst for these round-robin conversations. Lillie recounts her own response to *Beloved* and the connection among feelings, language, conversation, and understanding:

> I don't think I understood it all, not intellectually. But all my feelings got it. It touched every feeling I'd ever had. Every minute little feeling, even vague ones, it touched. So when I finished reading it, I understood that book in terms of my feelings. But in terms of how it all fits together on an intellectual level, if I had to analyze it, I'd be a little lost. I

can talk about emotions, how I felt about everything that happened. *It gets clearer as I talk about it* [my emphasis]. That's what's books do. They touch feelings, and then I have to find words for the feelings. The only way I can find words for feelings is to talk about it with lots of people, because they often have the words that I'm looking for.

Sometimes the books give me the words. Or they will give me the situation, a picture. The picture helps. It begins to make the feeling clearer until I find the words. The words make the feelings very clear when I can find the language for the feeling. I still have to do the feeling. In doing the feelings, sometimes I have to be patient. So the words become important in terms of being able to share the feelings, and also to find some ease with the feeling in terms of understanding it. Language seems very important in terms of that.

This explanation calls to mind James Pennebaker's explanation, which I cited in chapter 2, of the healing affect of language on people who had suffered some trauma: That putting inchoate feelings into words, into sentences, imposes an order on something that may at first seem bewildering and confusing. It is similar as well to Tommie's sense of the importance of "finding [one's] own language." For Lilly, recognizing and understanding feelings, which one does through language, through talk, seems vitally important. But the conversations about the books seem to me to go further than individual articulation of feelings. In talk about the books, the women establish and reinforce relationships with one another. In these relationships, they practice speaking out, gaining experience in what bell hooks calls "talking back," which she defines as "speaking as an equal, . . . daring to disagree, . . . having an opinion" (*Talking Back* 5). According to Lilly, when someone in the group has read a book that "touches feelings," that person lends the book to someone else; when the second woman has read it, these two begin the talk about the book. As others read it, they join the conversation, in pairs, in threes or fours, speaking with one another with "the intimacy and intensity" of "woman speech" that hooks claims as the source her own voice and authorship (*Talking Back* 6). Lilly describes this:

> What happens is that recovery is a part of all of that discussion even though it isn't the main focus of the discussion. It seems to help the recovery grow because the feelings have been touched by whatever it is that's been read. But it might take two years before it makes it around to everybody, because people work and have kids and are busy. People have become friends. We're no longer just in recovery together, but we've moved past that to a communion of friendship. That has changed how recovery works. You'd have these incredible conversations, like spider webs, going in this direction and then off down there. But they always ended up having a huge circle at the end. And it could take weeks for that conversation to be completed because you would only get a half hour here, an hour there. So it helped in terms of patience, too.

A specific example of how this process works comes in Lilly's report of the group's reading of Alice Walker's *Temple of My Familiar:*

> The husband and wife were close. Any time he read something that was important—I love this—she would read it because she wanted to know what was important to him. And every time she read something that was important, she would give it to him, but he would never read it. There ended up being a stack next to his desk of these books that were very important to her that he was going to read and that he never read. She finally saw the stack of books, and she realized that was a little murder. He loved her and was very interested in what she was interested in but not enough to read the books.
>   This idea of little murders in relationships hit me real

hard. I had all kinds of feelings about that, and I wanted to talk about it, and so I gave it to Tommie and, uh, somebody else. And that concept was really important for all of us. We all started talking about how positive finding little murders was, but how you can take it into a negative if you begin to see everything in terms of little murders. Are we then saying that happens in relationships? What *do* we share? What is it in terms of kindness and courtesy with each other? Is it just *pleases* and *thank yous*, or is it reading the book if somebody says it was real important to them? So that was wonderful. That was the biggest thing we got from *Temple of My Familiar.*

The practice of reading and talking began very early in the Al-Anon experience of the Mountain City women, Lilly says, with Ntozake Shange's *for colored girls who have considered suicide when the rainbow is enuf*:

I saw [the play] in New York. And I literally carried it in my purse for years. It was the first thing that gave me the sense that it could get better, that something could help it get better. I started reading sections of it to people I got close to. Then [later] we would take turns reading it. One time we had a gathering of about six women. What was interesting was the comments about what people liked. Some of them liked the anger. Someone liked the one about the plant—leaving it on his door—'i am ending this affair' —and the assertiveness in terms of men—'you may water it yr damn self.' What one woman loved was Sechita, who loves all the attention and knows she's manipulated men, and they go home with her, but she wants them gone in the morning because she wants her life back in order the next morning.

I loved watching what people liked. And we talked a lot about it. It changed. The more conversation we added about it, the fuller everything got, because there were so many different ways to look at one poem, depending on who felt what from it. Then I got to using it in my lead, the last few lines: 'i found god in myself & i loved her/i loved her fiercely.' That was the impact of the whole book to me. And that's what I wanted to find. The lending started with that and it grew from that.

Interestingly, many of the books these women, all white, talked about specifically are by African American women: Walker's *The Color Purple* and *The Temple of My Familiar,* Morrison's *Beloved,* and Shange's *for colored girls.* Part of this may be situational: the interviews took place in the early nineties, about the time Walker and Morrison were selling well and receiving attention in the popular press. But the attraction to these books likely goes beyond the bestseller list. One obvious reason is the strength—sometimes assertiveness—of the women characters, who survive oppression and brutality. Another is the theme of spirituality as a source of confidence, rarely a theme in fiction by contemporary white women. Another is the images of women in community offering healing to one another. The fiction of African American women writers seems, in Sicherman's words, to "extend the range of the possible" for these white women (216).

Indeed the content of these novels may be said to parallel the experience of the Mountain City women: overcoming adversity through a spiritual change fostered by a fellowship of supportive women. According to feminist psychotherapists Jean Baker Miller and Irene Pierce Stiver in *The Healing Connection: How Women Form Relationships in Therapy and in Life,* "mutually empathic" relationships foster both emotional and cognitive development. Miller and Stiver, both affiliated with the Wellesley Centers for Women, argue against the traditional model of separation, or individuation, as the end point of healthy psychological development, asserting instead that "connections—the experience of mutual engagement and empathy—provide the original and continuing sources of that growth" (3). They say that "mutual empathy leads to mutual empowerment" (30). But the power Miller and Stiver are talking about is not "power over others, directing and controlling them; it is 'power with,' a power that grows as it is used to empower others" (16). Such "mutually growth-fostering relationships" depend upon hearing and being heard, understanding and being understood, Miller and Stiver say (19).

According to Miller and Stiver's critique, a patriarchal culture like ours mitigates against women receiving this sort of empathy and empowerment:

> While many men have received a great deal of empathy that has helped them become empowered, often they have not been aware of it. . . . At the same time most women have not received from men the same empathic attention to their experience nor the support for their actions that would flow from mutually empathic interactions. (37)

Imbalanced relationships disempower when "disconnection" rather than "connection" occurs, according to Miller and Stiver. Disconnection is not unusual in alcoholic families, and family members consequently suffer from the usual list of symptoms that manifest with isolation, Miller and Stiver assert. They argue that Twelve-Step groups often provide relationships wherein women find "powerful connections and validation" (182). Indeed, Miller and Stiver have found these groups so effective in fostering growth that in *The Healing Connection* they speak out against critics who "reveal a lack of contact with the many people who have experienced the powerful beneficial effects of some of these groups   [W]e believe that some recent writers have underestimated the profound help that can be provided by a good mutual help group" (183).

Asserting that connections with others help people become "strong, active initiators and responders" (52), Miller and Stiver seem to be describing how the "communion of friendship" works among the Mountain City Al-Anon women. Miller and Stiver say that "respond[ing] to another person's feelings with feelings of their own, regardless of what the feelings themselves are" is both pleasurable and significant (35). Recognizing someone else's feelings, feeling *with* the other person, empowers not only the speaker, who is taken seriously, acknowledged, and therefore affirmed, but also the hearer, who in taking seriously, acknowledging, and affirming another, has an effect on the speaker. Having an effect on another human being is, to be sure, the most basic definition of power. It is this response—not just to texts but to one another—that contextualizes the Mountain City women's reading. To use Rosenblatt's terms, the Mountain City Al-Anon women prefer to read aesthetically, but this aesthetic experience includes talk of the women's emotional responses as well.

According to Miller and Stiver, when connections between human beings are established, even when the connections occur outside the primary relationship, the negative symptoms that grow out of destructive relationships diminish (80). This is what happens with the Mountain City Al-Anon women, both in the formal meetings and in the informal, unstructured conversations that occur outside the meetings. In experiencing the reading of *for colored girls,* for example, the women also experience "feeling with" one another. Aesthetic reading, we learn, is not, then, just an individual practice but a social one as well. The Al-Anon women pay attention to one another's emotional responses and offer validation. For example, when Lilly says that the women discussed the notion of "little murders" in relationships after the reading of Walker's *The Temple of My Familiar,* she is telling us that these women recognized as important one another's feelings and thoughts about what it means to be in a relationship. They shared with one another their own experiences and together used the concept to try to articulate a set of reasonable expectations and moral guidelines (though not rules) for behavior in relationships. Clearly, the women involved in these conversations had an effect on one another. Such talk is nurturing, and, therefore, according to Miller and Stiver, empowering.

In this discussion of reading there is very little talk of the ways of reading typically required in literature classes. Indeed, the reading that the Mountain City women do, which privileges response, has long been dismissed as anti-intellectual, emotional, or sentimental. The Mountain City women's readings exemplify what generations of literary critics have called "the affective fallacy." In the "Common Properties" article, Gere points to the disparity between the club-women's reading and school, but she could just as well be describing the reading of the Mountain City women.

Gere's research shows that the members of women's clubs found their relationships with one another enhanced by the common reading but more so by the conversation, which allowed many interpretations, not just one. Gere calls this kind of reading "subversive," quoting the apparatus of a literature textbook from the turn of the twentieth century to demonstrate that schools and colleges at the time made little room for affective responses and variations from the "right" answer (388). According to Gere,

> In insisting on the possibility of pleasure, of "liking" a text, members of the Friday Club demonstrate an affective investment in the system of signification and allow for a multiplicity of meanings to emerge from that signification. In so doing, they disrupt the "classroom" intellect of the dominant culture. (390)

In literary reading, the point has been, by and large, to see a relationship between verbal structures and ideas. The Mountain City women read to see relationships between the text and their lives. In their circle, what the women feel and say and think is valued more than some mythical "correct" reading: "The more conversation we added about it, the fuller everything got, because there were so many ways to look at one poem." For them, school reading, literary reading, becomes an irrelevancy. In this group of women, reading is a matter of life, and interpretation—meaning—begins with feeling and is something to be shared, discussed, and questioned, not for abstract, intellectual, cognitive, or artistic reasons but for immediate, personal, spiritual, and social ones. The conversation about the texts they read creates what Lilly calls a communion of friendship, where the Mountain City women use literacy and orality to form and re-form voice and self as they practice everyday life.

4 / Power as Positive and Available

In her article "Literacy in Three Metaphors," Sylvia Scribner could almost be describing the reading and writing of the Mountain City Al-Anon women: "The single most compelling fact about literacy is that it is a *social* achievement" (72, her emphasis). Scribner explains that despite the widely held assumption that literacy is an attribute of individuals, human beings acquire their abilities with literacy "only in the course of participation in socially organized activities with written language" (72). Certainly, as we have seen, the Mountain City women's literate practices aimed at spiritual growth occur within a rich social context. For these women—to continue with Scribner's words—"individual literacy is relative to social literacy" (72).

Deborah Brandt makes a similar point as she demonstrates that the particular reading and writing of individuals depend upon the sponsors of their literacy—that is, the agencies, groups, organizations, institutions that invite or require people to read and write ("Sponsors"). As the sponsors of literacy vary—parents, siblings, spouses, children, friends, schools, communities, clubs, religious organizations, unions, businesses, industry—so, too, do the function, use, and attributes of literacy acquired by groups and individuals. The abilities acquired with literacy are tied specifically to the functions for which the literacy is used, as Scribner and coauthor Michael Cole demonstrate in their "Unpacking Literacy" article. In research among the Vai people of northern Africa, Scribner and Cole found that those literate in Arabic generally performed better on specific serial memory tasks because reading in Arabic is used primarily for memorizing the Qur'an; the Vai literates who had acquired English in Western-type schools were better at what we define as abstract reasoning because along with the reading lessons came lessons in the kinds of textual reasoning valued in the West.

Given the social nature of literacy, then, viewing the Mountain City women's uses of reading and writing as only individual practices would impoverish our understanding of what their literacy is, what purposes it is put to, and how it works in their lives. The Mountain City women's literacy is shaped, disciplined, invited, and constrained by their participation in the Al-Anon group. This literacy is therefore aimed at the attainment of inner peace, personal growth, and emotional maturity, all attributes of the Al-Anon conception of spirituality. Yet, the Mountain City women's literacy, both individually and collectively, is shaped, disciplined, invited, and constrained by the traditions and practices of the larger society as well. That is to say, while the literacy of the women who talked with me is sponsored by their Al-Anon group in their particular historical time and place, it is, or has been, sponsored, as well, by other institutions—schooling during childhood, adolescence, and adulthood; the roles of women in families, marriage, and society; religion; and the workplace. All these reinscribe the kinds of behaviors, including literate behaviors, acceptable for women in our culture.

To reflect on the literate practices of the Mountain City women, I organize this chapter primarily around the three metaphors of literacy identified by Scribner—literacy as state of grace, literacy as adaptation, and literacy as power. Along the way, I show how the aesthetic reading and the private writing among the Mountain City Al-Anon women complicate Scribner's more public categories. Such private, hidden, or "vernacular" literate practices, according to David Barton and Mary Hamilton in *Local Literacies: Reading and Writing in One Community,* are "not regulated by the rules and procedures of dominant social institutions and . . . have their origins in everyday life" (247). Vernacular literacies, Barton and Hamilton say, are often "less valued by society[, and] . . . learned informally" (254). The Al-Anon women's vernacular literacies are, I believe, more important to the re-forming of their identities than their public literacies. I argue finally that these new identities, though private or vernacular themselves, are in fact political, indicating that perhaps the academy needs to widen its conception of power to include what Cornel West calls the politics of conversion.

Three Metaphors and a Complication

Our deepest beliefs about the value and importance of reading and writing can be found, Scribner explains, in three metaphors, each one "rooted in certain assumptions about the social motivations for literacy in this country, the nature of existing literacy practices, and judgments about which practices are critical for individual and social enhancement" (73). The literacy-as-adaptation metaphor points to the "survival or pragmatic value" of reading and writing (73). Here we find talk of "functional literacy," which Scribner defines as "the level of proficiency necessary for effective performance in a range of settings and customary activities" (73). Literacy as adaptation includes the kinds of skills with reading and writing demanded by the economic system, which, these days, includes technology, as Cynthia L. Selfe points out in her recent *Technology and Literacy in the Twenty-First Century*. This is the kind of literacy that politicians and school boards call for, and it is often measured in grade level, words per minute, and comprehension scores on standardized tests. Necessary to many, if not most, jobs in a postindustrial capitalist culture, literacy for survival is akin to Rosenblatt's efferent reading, the reading that one does while directing his or her attention outward "toward concepts to be retained, ideas to be tested, actions to be performed *after* the reading" (24, my emphasis). In the vernacular sense, literacy as adaptation includes all those kinds of reading and writing necessary to keep a household going— reconciling bank statements, paying bills, corresponding with bureaucracies, keeping calendars and schedules, following recipes, writing instructions for family members, writing notes and cards to family and friends, sending messages to school with children, and so forth.

The second metaphor, literacy as power, according to Scribner, "emphasizes the relationship of literacy and group or community advancement" (75). This is why literacy in some societies is re-stricted or limited to an elite group—priests and scribes, the church, the higher social classes. Here is the pride in "my son the doctor" or "my daughter the teacher"—the family member who has attained with help from advanced literacy a position of power or status in the community, thereby marking the upward movement of the family or group. But also included is the notion of "literacy as an instrument for human liberation and social change" (75). The literacy-as-power metaphor embraces literacy as a protector of civil rights and eco-nomic opportunity. This is the literacy promised by the modernist narrative of liberty, which I identify in my "Narratives of Literacy" article as the first Freire narrative. This is the literacy that we in composition studies have in mind when we talk about our first-year college students as if they were Freire's third-world adult learners or assume Freire's methods transfer neatly to the complex cultural, ethnic, social, and economic mix of the United States. Later in this chapter, I discuss the distinction made by the Mountain City women between political and spiritual, or personal, power, arguing that the vernacular literacy the women practice in their Al-Anon program works to bring about a kind of vernacular power but power nonetheless.

The third metaphor Scribner posits is literacy as state of grace or salvation, though she immediately calls both labels "unsatisfac-tory because they give a specific religious interpretation . . . to the tendency in many societies to endow the literate person with special virtues" (76–77). Sometimes, the literacy-as-state-of-grace meta-phor means, according to Scribner, knowledge of sacred books, such as the Bible or the Qur'an but in our secular society, as she points out, it often means Culture with a capital C—that is, poetry or philosophy—or intellectual development, the ability to use sym-bols to solve abstract problems (77). Culture is what E. D. Hirsch Jr. means when he talks about literacy—knowledge, chiefly, of par-ticular texts or historical facts. Intellectual development and so-called abstract problem solving are the end points of the Havelock-Ong great leap literacy narrative, which I identify as the modernist narrative as cognition ("Narratives of Literacy"). The literacies de-

scribed by both Hirsch and Eric Havelock are politically conservative, allying reading and writing with study requiring leisure and
therefore wealth, a relationship noted since at least 55 B.C.E. in
Cicero's comments on time, literacy, and rhetoric in *Of Oratore* 1.17
(211). Despite Scribner's quick dismissal of the spiritual in favor of
the secular, the Mountain City women show, in the little narrative I
have related in chapters 2 and 3, that, in addition to its metaphorical value, literacy for some people—for themselves—is literally a
means to grace.

The spiritual grace attained through informal, vernacular reading and writing with their Al-Anon friends is not knowledge of sacred texts (though that certainly comes) but rather according to the
Mountain City women, "confidence," "self-esteem," and "belief in
myself," which they, in turn, identify as a kind of power even while
denying the public, political implications of that word. When they
talk about literacy as adaptation—for example, for Judy a job as
part-time manager of a supermarket and for Jill a college degree
and plans for graduate school—they talk more in terms of spirituality than of literacy. For these women, their vernacular experiences and literacies take priority over their public experiences and
literacies.

State of Grace

In the state-of-grace metaphor, Scribner explains, literacy "tran-
scends" boundaries of political or economic power: "[T]he literate individual's life derives its meaning and significance from intellectual, aesthetic, and spiritual participation in the accumulated
creations and knowledge of humankind, made available through
the written word" (77). Interestingly, Scribner's juxtaposition of
the words *intellectual, aesthetic, spiritual,* and *participation* evoke
Rosenblatt's aesthetic reading, where the focus is on the inner experience of the reader *during* the reading. Drawing on John Dewey,
Rosenblatt explains that an aesthetic experience is

> simply the stuff of ordinary day-to-day experience defined,
> *heightened,* complete. . . . If there is an aesthetic element in

day-to-day life, it depends on a certain *shift* of interest, attention, or *awareness,* from the purely practical or referential to the immediately experienced qualitative aspects. (37, my emphasis)

The Mountain City women use similar terms in their discussions of spirituality. When I asked, for example, for an explanation of the term "spiritual awakening," a phrase that occurs in the Twelfth Step and makes frequent appearances in the women's discourse, the Mountain City women invariably defined it as a change in understanding or perception: "The world shifted, got brighter," Jen says. As they talked about this shift in viewpoints, they invariably used narratives to explain a spiritual experience as a heightened awareness of the ordinary. In many, if not most, cases, the stories they told keyed in on their literate practices. Lilly, we remember, says that the first glimmer of hope that things could get better for her came from reading Shange's *for colored girls who have considered suicide when the rainbow is enuf.* Judy describes her spiritual awakening in terms of her understanding of two particular texts, the ODAT and chapter 8 in the Big Book, her spiritual growth as nurtured by her reading, and her achievement of peace in terms of a text she herself wrote, the essay published in *In All Our Affairs.* Jill, on the other hand, locates her spirituality first in talk with other Al-Anon members but also in her writing, describing her Fourth Steps as exercises that change her views and allow for acceptance and her journals as life records that ultimately effect gratitude.

Judy's spiritual awakening is associated in her memory with her ability to "read" *One Day at a Time* and the chapter called "To the Wives" in AA's Big Book. Judy, as we have seen, read chapter 8 of the Big Book shortly after her husband returned from treatment. She reports: "The only thing I got out of it was: Don't piss him off, he'll get drunk. That's not what it says at all. But that's all I could get out of it at the time." Several months later, Judy went to her first Al-Anon meeting, where, she says, she heard that she was not the cause of the misery she had lived in for the previous ten years. With this information, she says, her perception of reality changed. She identifies this message as her "initial spiritual awakening." The result was that over the course of her first month in Al-Anon, Judy learned to read the ODAT in different ways; recall that Judy said that on first reading she hadn't "understood a damn word of it." Now Judy identifies being able to read the ODAT with understanding, not as part of her enculturation into the group, as I might, but as part of her spiritual awakening:

> Everything I read in the ODAT book I could understand. It was like God said, "You're no longer foreign. You can understand what you're reading." Of course I didn't understand it like I do nine years later. But at least if it didn't make sense, I'd ask. It was a whole different ball game for me. I got the growth through reading. And chapter 8, "To the Wives," started to mean something real different.

Jill defines her spiritual awakenings as "awarenesses of myself," explaining, "They've been real painful. My sponsor says that they don't have to be painful. But so far the ones that I've been aware of, that have been real big, have come with a lot of sadness and a lot of pain. And healing." Like the other women who talked with me, Jill uses a narrative to illustrate this abstraction. The story she tells centers on her experience with an Al-Anon friend who had been arrested a second time for writing bad checks. Jill says she had to face first her disillusionment and anger and then her self-righteousness. She concludes the story:

> Where the spiritual awakening came was in terms of my perception. I would never have been able to see the expectations of my friend that I had, had I not been in that much pain. I might have gone on saying, "Well, wasn't it nice that I helped this person?" giving myself a pat on the back. "She's doing real well." But after all this talking and writing, I was able to go see her and give her some Snicker bars and a carton of cigarettes and tell her how I felt but not with the judgment that I had had before. I could tell her

how sad I was this had happened to her and tell her that I couldn't bail her out again.

Taking the opportunity to talk about her spiritual progress, Jill continues: "The talking that I do with my sponsor is real important in my spiritual program, because I find myself saying things that I don't know I felt, or saying things that I don't know were there until they came out. And I do that just by talking." Similarly, Jill finds writing to be important in the shift of perception entailed in a spiritual awakening. She describes an early Fourth Step:

> It was thirty pages. I remember telling my sponsor, I don't have any resentments, I don't resent anything. I thought I was happy and optimistic. She said, "Think of one person that you really have a resentment against." It was my ex-husband. I thought, I'm still pissed off at him. And as I wrote these resentments down for him, they triggered everybody else's. It just flowed. It was just like an out-pouring.

Getting resentment "out" is a way of getting past it, Jill says, bringing about a change in her world, her reality. For Jill, as we have seen, her written Fourth-Step form is a useful way to separate her feelings and responsibilities from those of other people, a move she finds necessary to her own growth. That the Mountain City women identify such a shift in perception as spiritual explains their preference for aesthetic reading—the kind of reading that has the possibility of engendering an inner experience that alters one's world view.

In addition to writing Fourth Steps as a way to achieve spiritual peace or healing, the Mountain City women use their personal writing as a means of acceptance and forgiveness, two other paths to the shift in perception the Al-Anon women call spiritual. For the women who talked with me, forgiveness is not just of other persons but of themselves as well. Forgiveness changes their view of themselves. As bell hooks explains, "Our capacity to forgive allows us to be in touch with our own agency (that is the power to act on our own behalf to change a situation)" (*Sisters of the Yam* 167). Learning to perceive themselves differently is such an important part of the Mountain City women's journey that some of them save their writing as records of this process. Catherine, recall, keeps her "spiral notebooks," valuing them as a sign of her emotional and spiritual journey, which she does not intend to destroy but rather leave as legacy of herself for her daughters to find. Judy says, "I've kept everything I've written. And I've dated them so I can go back and look at them and know where I was at that point in time. I go back and read them." Tommie keeps her writing, especially her "prose" and her Dear God letters, which she shares with people she sponsors. Jill gives a more explicit explanation of why keeping such writings is important, saying that seeing her former self on the page allows her "to grieve for that person that was there, that me that was there, and . . . feel very grateful that my higher power had brought me through that. I like seeing me down there. It makes me real."

For the Mountain City women, literacy as state of grace is not an isolated occurrence but rather part of habitual reading and writing for spiritual growth. They read and write virtually every day, as we have seen, not for spiritual band-aids, but, instead, with the purpose of changing their minds—changing their hearts, the Mountain City women would say. To complicate simple measures of literacy, John Oxenham introduces the issue of permanence, wondering whether temporary abilities with reading and writing ought to "count" in measures of literacy. For the Mountain City women, reading and writing for spiritual purposes seems a permanent part of their lives. Their purpose is not to become experts on the texts of Al-Anon but rather to change their own perceptions, to shift their attention, to attain a spiritual awakening.

But even while describing their own reading and writing for state of grace, the Mountain City women deny the necessity of literacy for spiritual growth. Literacy may make spiritual development easier for some people, but it isn't necessary, they argue. Drawing parallels between reading and listening and between writing and talking, they assert that people can listen to AA or Al-Anon tapes instead of reading and can talk to a sponsor or other program friends instead of writing. What they believe is necessary for sustained spiritual growth, though not to particular spiritual insights (which certainly can and do occur spontaneously to individuals), is the talk that goes on in the communion of friendship. Their comments that literacy is not necessary to the program may signal the denial of their own privilege as literates in a region where literacy rates among the poor, the working class, and rural folk are lower than the national average. Jill said once that she was fearful that newcomers might be uncomfortable in Al-Anon meetings because "we are all so eloquent." The others steadfastly deny that the lack of education might prevent participation in the group, perhaps another iteration of the program ideology that social class does not exist. Despite the complicating and still unexplored issue of class, I agree with the Mountain City women that literacy is enabling, not causal; helpful, not essential. The spiritual practices the women engage in—seeking spiritual insight and examining one's self—are not exclusive to literates or to middle-class people. Untold numbers have, and have had, rich, intentional spiritual lives without using reading or writing. But in Al-Anon, at least in Al-Anon in Mountain City, reading and writing are ways to participate in a spiritual journey.

Power

The personal development of the Mountain City women indicates that the literacy they engage in for spiritual growth has in fact been empowering. According to Scribner,

> The literacy-as-power metaphor emphasizes a relationship
> between literacy and group or community advancement. . . .
> [E]xpansion of literacy skills is often viewed as a means for
> poor and politically powerless groups to claim their place
> in the world. (75)

In the Mountain City women's accounts of their literacy, I contend, we see the "advancement" of one group of women; we see these women "claim[ing] their place in the world." We see, I submit, literacy as power. But this is not how my research participants look at it, perhaps because they share a female reluctance to claim or desire power, and *power* is, unfortunately, the word I used to solicit their thoughts on this topic.

Power having been traditionally denied them, women generally and the Mountain City women in particular have learned, often explicitly, that power is unwomanly, unfeminine, even cruel. Because women have been on the receiving end, they are often suspicious of power, even when they don't quote Lord Acton's comment about its corrupting influence. But because the Eleventh Step explicitly mentions power as one of the rewards of a spiritual life—"Sought through prayer and meditation to improve our conscious contact with God *as we understood Him,* praying only for knowledge of His will and the power to carry that out"—I inquired about whether the women saw intersections of literacy, spirituality, and power. Judy refused to talk about literacy as power; the only power she has, she says, is spiritual:

> I consider the power in the program a power of your own making. I consider the power out there, of the rich and famous, that's a whole different power. The power that we have in the program comes within us. We have the power to carry that [God's will] out. Power comes from confidence, power comes from belief, comes from doing.

Judy seems here to be making a useful distinction between political power and spiritual power, one that I first ran across in M. Scott Peck's best-selling *The Road Less Traveled: A New Psychology of Love, Traditional Values, and Spiritual Growth:*

> Political power is the capacity to coerce others, overtly or covertly to do one's will. This capacity resides in a position such as a kingship or presidency, or else in money. It does not reside in the person who occupies the position or

possesses the money. . . . Spiritual power, however, resides
entirely within the individual and has nothing to do with
the capacity to coerce others. . . . It is the capacity to make
decisions with maximum awareness. It is consciousness.
(284–85)

Jill makes this same distinction: "I don't feel that I have to have
power over someone else; it could be misused that way. But it's more
of a self-power that I get. Maybe that's why it's helped my self-
esteem." This is the distinction that we saw in the Jean Baker Miller
and Irene Pierce Stiver discussion in chapter 3. When Miller and
Stiver talk about "mutually empowering" connections, the power
they are talking about is not "power over others, directing and controlling them; it is 'power with,' a power that grows as it is used to
empower others" (16). Jill explains the paradoxical nature of the
spiritual power she has achieved:

> When I am able to let go of what I think is right and wrong
> and be okay where I'm at and trust that I'm going to be
> okay one way or the other, then I have power. I don't have
> fear. I have serenity. I can do things I need to do for myself
> and my family. Because I'm not constantly in tomorrow
> worrying about what's going to happen. The giving up of
> power empowers me, and that does not make sense.

But unlike Judy, Jill does go on to connect power with literacy
explicitly:

> Literacy empowers me—self-empowers. As a woman. First
> of all, because I am no longer hopeless or helpless. That I
> can do these things—in education, and I'm not only talk-
> ing about my education at the university, but how I choose
> to educate myself about incest and or how I choose to edu-
> cate myself on the disease of alcoholism. These things are
> empowering for me as a person.

This point leads Jill to see a connection among literacy, spirituality, and power:

> If you can read something other than your own experience and you can learn from it, you have more options or more things to choose from. Before I came into the program, I didn't know options and choices. I thought my marriage needed to be this way, based on what my grandmother was telling me. Then going into the program and reading the literature, things were given to me, even brought to me from the outside, that I could use which then empowered me.

Similarly, Jen admits that she has more power now than previously, but only "power in the sense that I feel I'm more effective. I have more persistence. I'm more assertive. I believe that tapping into my inner power, my higher power, is where that comes from." But after several minutes of denying that literacy had anything to do with that power, she concedes that her literacy level is part of her power. After musing on how sometimes level of thought and language correlates with the level of reading, she concludes reluctantly that education "would definitely affect someone's power." Yet she makes it clear she is talking here about political power, not power in the Eleventh-Step sense.

Tommie seems more willing than the others to admit to owning power. But although she does not explicitly draw the distinction between personal or spiritual power and political power that the others make, she seems to use those categories implicitly:

> The kind of power I used [before the program] had hurt people. My perception when I came to the program was that I had to accept that I was powerless and that I was always going to be. But then a light came through, through Lilly. She's the first person I heard talking about power as positive and available. She said you got it back in the Third Step ["Made a decision to turn our will and our lives

over to the care of God *as we understood Him*"]. Then you tap your own power. It was a new concept to me that I could have power. [Before,] I didn't see making decisions as power.

But making decisions about one's life is the most basic kind of power, though certainly a power prohibited to most women. For most women throughout history and for most women in the world today, other people make the basic life decisions. Even in Western countries where women have remarkably more civil rights than previously, important decisions are still made by important people, and women are often considered unimportant—by the culture, by government officials, by religious leaders, by artists and critics, by academic disciplines, by families, by husbands, by the men (and sometimes the women) they work for. Tommie explains that her "disease"—that is, what brought her to Al-Anon in the first place—was doing what other people told her to; before the program, she says, "I didn't know I had a choice." Reading and writing and talking, the Mountain City women learn they have choices.

Sometimes, for the Mountain City women, power is instantiated in choosing to speak to the one person the women have seen as most powerful in their lives: their husbands. Recall Catherine's comment to her husband: Where once she would have remained silent, she said, "Paul, I am trying to tell you something about me." Judy's narrative about her first Al-Anon meeting includes coming home and saying to her husband, "Get your coffee and come here." When he sat down, she reports, she looked him in the eye and said, "We in Al-Anon look, I don't care if you go out that door and get drunk, it's not my fault." Judy's moment of victory was short lived, however, when, as she remembers, Jack replied, "Yes, I know that." Nonetheless, this was a woman who for weeks had been assuring her husband that everything was "fine" despite consuming anger about the past and paralyzing fear of the future.

This coming to voice is, as hooks says, "a revolutionary gesture . . . especially relevant for women who are speaking or writing for the first time" (*Talking Back* 12). The transformation of silence into language is, as Audre Lorde argues, a victory over oppressive forces that silence members of marginal groups. Through their spiritual and literate practices, the Mountain City women have learned to speak. But as Lilly explains, it isn't literacy that allows people to speak, and it isn't educational level or attainment of the approved speech forms. According to Lilly, "People don't just speak. They have to be listened to first. I don't care what your language is like. If nobody's listened, you won't speak." Peter Elbow phrases it somewhat differently in *Writing with Power:*

> The wild child brought up only by animals in the woods does not speak at all. Any "back to the basics" movement in the teaching of writing needs to start by ensuring each child the most basic thing of all: a real audience for his written words—an audience that really listens and takes the interchanges seriously. (184)

An audience—the connection between human beings—is central to the development of voice—of the ability to name the world—according to Miller and Stiver in *The Healing Connection*. The connection between human beings is also the basis for Freire's pedagogy of the oppressed. Literacy is not, for Freire, merely decoding or encoding; it is rather using letters, sounds, words to name the world, not just for oneself but to others as well. Miller and Stiver call on feminist therapists to serve as this connection, this audience, for women whose disconnection from the significant people in their lives has robbed them of their ability to speak; Freire asks teachers to listen as students tell their individual and cultural stories and to provide students with the technology to tell those stories. The vernacular literacies of the Mountain City Al-Anon women in their spiritual search—"hybrid practices which draw on a range of practices from different domains" (Barton and Hamilton 247)—foster these healing connections. The women who talked with me come to voice by means of the talk that goes on in response to their reading and writing. This is, I argue, literacy for power.

Adaptation

The last metaphor Scribner offers is literacy as adaptation. This
category includes the reading and writing we do for survival, for
pragmatic and economic uses, for functioning in our particular
worlds. This is the literacy that, in fact, was the main skill required
for the work that Catherine, Jennifer, and Jill were doing at the
time of the interviews. For Catherine, the bookstore was interesting work because it allowed her to read and talk about a variety
of books with college-town customers. And reading and writing
at fairly high levels were, as we have seen, part of both Jennifer's
and Jill's work as students at the university. Yet, not surprisingly,
the Mountain City women attribute their "adaptation" more to
their spiritual growth than to their literacy. Even when they are
talking about the reading and writing involved in their jobs, literacy is not, for these women, something separate from their spirituality.

Recall Jennie's comments in chapter 2 about how she writes
more effectively for her classes now that she lets her words come
from "somewhere other than my thinking." In this comment, Jennifer attributes the quality of her work not to her literacy but to her
spiritual growth—to a newfound trust in her own abilities. She has
learned, further, that her task as a student is not merely to please the
professor or impress her classmates but to make meaning for herself for her own purposes and then share it, unafraid. This is not
something that had been part of Jennifer's understanding of school
literacy. In Jen's world, school and self had been disconnected. For
Jennifer, as for other research participants, literacy learning had
been, as Barton and Hamilton point out, separated from use; school
is mere practice, not the real thing. Yet at this point, Jennie is able
to "integrate" the two activities—public, school-sponsored writing and a vernacular, private practice (Barton and Hamilton 252).
What Jennie had previously written in school had had little rele-
vance to her life. But by the time she began graduate school, Jennifer was so accustomed to writing for meaning as part of her

Al-Anon program that this purpose began to impose itself on her school writing as well. We see here a rich example of a vernacular literacy changing a dominant, or officially sanctioned, literacy. As Barton and Hamilton explain, vernacular literacies "often underpin and support the development of more [culturally] valued literacies" (255).

Jill talks about her literacy for adaptation in terms of goals:

> I'm going to go on to graduate school. I graduate in December and I'm going to apply for spring if I can. I might have to wait a semester because I want to get in that [family studies] program. I'm going to get my Ph.D. That's a goal. I almost feel that I'm pushing my luck by saying that, but I can have a goal.

Jill's spiritual power has given her, she claims, the courage to go back to school and do the required work without being hampered by fear: "I've noticed in this English class I'm taking, I'm not agonizing. [Once,] I would have everybody in the house miserable. If I had to write a paper, I would rant and rave and stomp around. I don't have to do that now."

Though Tommie was not working at a paid job at the time of the interviews, she was "looking out for" her mother, who was in a nursing home. Tommie discounts reading and writing in connection with this task as "not a big deal so far." But Tommie is clear that before the program she would not have been able to cope with this situation: "I would have told my family members, I can't do this, you do it. And I'd have disappeared." Though dealing with social workers and medical-care providers is not—at least not yet—a part of Tommie's literacy for adaptation, her ability to do what she needs to do for her family is something she attributes to her program-generated belief in her own abilities. I would argue that Tommie is able to "protect [her mother's] dignity" because the literate practices that are part of Tommie's Al-Anon program have enabled her to establish a sense of her own worth and to find her own language. I surmise that any number of hidden—virtually invisible—literacy events are part of Tommie's new role—keeping track of doctor's appointments, checking on medications, making informal notes on changing conditions, and so forth; such activities are part of the vernacular literacies we all engage in and depend on to survive in our complex culture.

Judy's experience in going to work part-time at a large supermarket in Mountain City may be closer to what Scribner calls literacy for adaptation. But in the end, Judy, too, attributes her success not to literacy but to the character she has developed from working her Al-Anon program:

> I went to Smith's Supermarket and filled out an application. I put a note on it: "I am a 38-year old housewife. I've been out of the workforce for seventeen years while raising my daughter. I'm happy-go-lucky, love people, and have a wonderful sense of humor. Please consider me. I'm hardworking, and I will show up." It was that note that got me the interview. Because I knew what I was capable of.
>
> I became an office cashier for the last six months I worked there. I had to take readings of how much was brought in all night. I had to do the break lists, schedules, newspapers ads. There was a lot of writing involved. In the beginning, it was scary, because I was not used to dealing with thousands and thousands of dollars. I thought when I got there, I cannot. I'd never done a computer in my life. I'm a high-school graduate and went to beauty school. But then after I worked on the floor for a year and got promoted, I got real confident. Because I was honest. I've found a lot of people are thieves. You can't take for granted that other people are honest. Once you become honest in this program, you are honest in every phase of your life.

For these women—and I do not claim that they are representative of any class or group—literacy for adaptation, that is, reading and writing to deal with the world and to function in it, rests upon a spiritual and personal power—serenity, confidence, "belief in myself"—that emerges from the literacy they engage in as a means to grace. Often in the theoretical or research literature, the process is the opposite: first literacy as adaptation; then literacy as power but usually power defined as economic and political; then literacy as state of grace but almost always described in nonspiritual terms such as cultural knowledge, self-fulfillment, or creativity. For the women who talked to me, vernacular forms of literacy result in spiritual power, which then work to undergird literacy as adaptation or literacy as political power.

The Personal Is the Political

In the little narrative of literacy I present here, the Mountain City women do transform—even liberate—themselves by means of spirituality and literacy, but they do so in a limited and local sense. Indeed, this is how genuine change happens, Cornel West says: "The politics of conversion proceeds principally on the local level— in those institutions in civil society still vital enough to promote self-worth and self-affirmation" (19). In the "Nihilism in Black America" essay, which was originally published in 1991 and to which I previously referred, West argues that the greatest threat to the black community in America is "the profound sense of psychological depression, personal worthlessness, and social despair" found particularly in inner-city neighborhoods (12–13). Reasons for this sense of hopelessness include the conditions under which African Americans have lived for hundreds of years in this country and "the cutthroat market morality devoid of any faith in deliverance or hope for freedom" that has weakened civil society in the black community (16). This sense of psychological depression and personal worthlessness is true, as well, of many women, I would argue, especially those in families with active alcoholism. Women, who also bear the weight of a history that has defined them as less than autonomous beings, live in a culture that can offer virtually nothing except market values. What is necessary for genuine change, West says, is not self-help programs or social analysis, though these are beneficial, but rather "a politics of conversion," "a turning of the soul," offering "hope for the future and meaning to struggle" (18–19). West believes that such a conversion comes through "an affirmation of one's worth—an affirmation fueled by the concern of others" (19): The task of oppressed people, therefore, is to come together to provide places where this "turning of the soul" might begin and might be nourished. The Mountain City women have done this through Al-Anon.

According to West and hooks, as we have seen, spiritual solutions can lead to political change—though probably not overnight and perhaps not in the form social critics would want. None of the Mountain City Al-Anon women divorces her husband or becomes a political activist. At the time of the interviews, Jennifer was divorced, and Catherine was separated, but neither woman had initiated the break-up. Tommie's husband was still drinking, and Jill's was newly sober, but neither woman had plans to leave—and indeed in the ensuing years, they have not. The material conditions of the Mountain City women's lives have not changed significantly, except that some of the children have grown up and moved away.

Lilly still "talks to people," does volunteer work at her sons' school, and travels, when she can get away, to far-away places with strange-sounding names. Tommie has undergone successful treatment for breast cancer and is working in the office at one of the medical clinics in Mountain City. Catherine and her husband divorced not long after the interviews; she is now retired, living in the same house, and visiting grandchildren and old friends. A few weeks after the first round of interviews, Judy moved with her husband to a town some sixty miles away from Mountain City. Her health has become precarious because of her diabetes, and so Judy no longer works outside the home. Recently, a large and noisy party in Mountain City celebrated her twentieth year in Al-Anon. Jennifer and Jill are social workers, sharing their wisdom with troubled families. Jill earned her masters degree. Jennifer finished hers and bought a house.

They all still attend Al-Anon, though perhaps not so intensely, being true oldtimers now. From time to time, one or two of them will hold office at the district and state levels of Al-Anon. They still talk to one another; they still pass books around the circle, which expands and contracts as other people come and go. As Lilly says, they have lives and kids and jobs, and so the circle is still informal, *ad hoc*. There have been no dramatic external transformations. Neither the literacy nor the spirituality of the Mountain City women accomplishes magic, though the women who talked with me believe that miracles occur in their lives on a daily basis.

Through what Al-Anon calls "a spiritual awakening," these women have, they assert, attained a kind of power that has improved their lives, though they attribute the changes to spiritual power more than to political power. Discussions of women and power lead inevitably to questions about feminism, and when I asked near the end of each interview whether the women considered themselves feminists, the answers were ambiguous. The problem seems to be, as it is for many of our female students, the label and the stereotype that go with it, a view nurtured by conservative politicians as well as the mainstream press. For example, Jill answered,

> If you use the negative term of a feminist as a woman real hard, then I'm not a feminist that way. But in terms of human dignity and specialness, then, yes, I'm a feminist. I feel real strongly a bond between women. And the program has given me that. Because women held my hand and brought me to where I'm at. And I want to reach out and do that for someone else.

Catherine's reply is similar: "No, I see [the term feminist] as militant. That may not be so at all. But I do want to come to the side of any woman who has been put down."

Lilly, who had worked for Amnesty International in New York in the sixties and seventies and whose station wagon in the early nineties still sported an ERA sticker, talked about feminism in ways that were surprisingly like those of the other women, despite her usual left-leaning political stances. The movement, she believed, had closed out women like her who had chosen not to work for pay outside the home. But her complaints went further, reflecting the Mountain City women's suspicion of political power:

I don't like coat hanger rallies. They're just like fetus rallies. It's the same. Let's not do the shock thing. I don't want
our vision to be only about how to get women somewhere.
I want the vision to be about how to get people together,
where men and women are equal. Power has to be shared
or it becomes a negative. I hate the term Feminist Majority.
Then a paternal power becomes a maternal power. What's
the bloody difference?

Tommie's stance is similar, though not as angry. After disavowing
"radical" feminism, Tommie says, "I heard the word *humanist* once,
and I liked that. But when I try to be a humanist, people call me a
feminist."

Judy understands the ambiguity in her own position, though in
some ways her view is much like that of the other women:

I enjoy the doors opening. But I am also very outspoken. I
generally say what I think, which gets me in trouble a lot.
I'm very dependent on my husband, though. But, like he
said when I went back to work, I'm not afraid now if something happens to him. I could go on. I know in the end I
would be okay. I know I have choices.

Whether these women are feminists depends on the definition.
If feminism is simply regarding women as fully human, as some
sage once put it, then these women are. If the definition includes
solidarity with other women or embraces the conviction that men
and women should share power or that women should and can have
choices in their own lives, then the Mountain City women are, certainly, feminists. However, they eschew aggressive public political
stances or declarations of superiority over other people including
but not limited to men, negative perceptions of feminism whose reality many academic women deny but that continue to flourish despite our protestations.

But the point is not how to define feminism. It is rather to
show that politics is an integral part of this little narrative of literacy, though it is not the overt, in-your-face variety that some in

composition studies appear to demand. The politics the Mountain City women practice may be revolutionary, but it is at the same time a domestic kind of politics—a vernacular politics, we might say. It takes place in private, in the home, in the family, in relationships with husbands, children, parents, siblings, friends. This politics is subtle, often hard for others to recognize. But it may well be the profoundest kind, because it is in families where fundamental change in the relations between men and women occurs, where, in fact, the next generation learns how power is to be used.

Indeed, it may be that in the academy our understanding of politics has been impoverished by seeing it as something that happens only in social critique employing a particular lexicon or in demonstrations in the street or at the polling booth. Perhaps the lesson here is that politics at its most basic is what happens between human beings—and that includes in classrooms and in employment practices in English departments. A more inclusive understanding of politics might offer a refreshing change. I, for one, have heard enough feminist-leftist analyses from academic men who continue to treat women colleagues as servants and from academic women who, aping their betters, accept the status quo. At any rate, the Mountain City Al-Anon women show us that the personal, the vernacular, even the spiritual, is political.

In the "Narratives of Literacy" article, I argued, following Ann Berthoff, that because North American academic readers have all too often missed the spiritual elements in Freire's pedagogy, composition studies has sometimes held a distorted view of his work. We have failed to see that while Freire is clearly concerned for the political, economic, and spiritual salvation of the oppressed, he is also interested in the spiritual salvation of the middle-class teachers. Because we didn't see the spiritual motivation for Freire's politics, we missed his most important lesson: Being treated as if one is worthy, as if one's life is important, as if what one has to say is significant and deserving attention, as if one is—yes—a fellow child of God allows some people, even the most silenced, to come to voice and, in so doing, to see the world and themselves differently.

5 / Literacy Lessons

What are we to learn from this study of actual women reading and writing for spiritual development? From chapter 4, two lessons seem evident, both of which expand our academic vision. First, if politics means acting in response to power, then the concept includes not just public statements or actions but also the personal, the domestic, as I argued in the previous chapter. While feminists assert that the personal is political, the left reasons that paying too close attention to our individual lives precludes the kinds of political activity that might bring about genuine social change. Certainly, intense focus on self means little time or energy to work to make society more equitable and just. But the domestic and the private, as bell hooks points out, sometimes must come first. And sometimes domestic, private change, as we have seen with the Mountain City women, is in itself political change, though generally hidden because domestic and private. In chapter 4, I argued that how we treat others is as much politics as what we say in public or how we vote.

The Mountain City women talk and listen to each other, empathize with one another, help each other think through problems, and so teach one another profound lessons about how human beings can treat each other and themselves. They learn from each other that it is possible to be agents in their own lives. The women who talked to me empower each other and, in turn, themselves "to choose with awareness, to change and adapt consciously, and in this sense to be able to have a share in determining their own destiny" (Coles 253). Similarly, we might see that students learn not just by what we say from behind a lectern or what we assign but by how we treat them, what we expect of them, what we allow—and help—them say or read or write.

A related lesson for me has been confirmation of Kenneth

Burke's "A way of seeing is a way of *not* seeing." I remind readers of my first impression of Tommie: Because she was insightful about the dynamics of the alcoholic family and articulate in a calm and even-toned way, I assumed she was a therapist, someone with advanced degrees. As I said in chapter 1, this judgment reveals far more about my biases, formed at least in part by the academy, than it does about Tommie. Later, when I went seeking information from people who did not claim to be experts, I learned a great deal. When I listened, the Mountain City women told me how literacy works in their lives. Paying attention to how actual people use reading and writing in a particular time and place for specific purposes, under specific material conditions, expands our academic views of literacy, of texts constructed and construed, and of the human beings who read and write.

The second lesson is that revisiting our notions of the spiritual and the religious might profit those of us in the academy. I hope that my work has shown that spirituality is as socially constructed as the fork and that taking seriously people's beliefs does not imply discussing or accepting a transcendent unchanging reality. It does mean accepting that people have beliefs and experiences they label spiritual or religious and that those beliefs and experiences play a significant roles in their lives. When whole areas of people's lives are closed off as unworthy of academic attention, the academy misses important information.

For language use to be effective, the whole person must be taken into account, as the Sophists taught. While asserting that the gods of the Greeks were many and ridiculous, the Sophists showed that effective rhetoric focuses not just on logos, or reason, and ethos, or the credibility of the rhetor, but also on pathos, not cheap emotion as rhetoric's critics attest but rather life-sustaining passion, deep feeling without which there is neither excellence nor purpose. The source of this passion is often found in religious or spiritual experience, which is always culturally and socially determined.

But there are other implications for our field, I think, in my study of the connections of literacy and spirituality. I organize this chapter around three categories of lessons—for theory, research, and pedagogy.

Theory

What might this work contribute to theoretical discussions of literacy? First, it indicates, as others have pointed out, that by itself literacy changes very little. In an essay I read almost twenty years ago, Johan Galtung put it like this:

> What would happen if the whole world became literate? Answer: not so very much, for the world is by and large structured in a way that it is capable of absorbing the impact. But if the whole world consisted of literate, autonomous, critical, constructive people, capable of translating ideas into action, individually or collectively, the world would change. (93)

Indeed as we have seen with both Tommie and Jill, reading can be a way not only *not* to change what is but a way to endure it. At one time in their lives, literacy supplied Tommie and Jill with effective escapes from life's problems. If my study shows anything that can be generalized, it is that the grand narratives of literacy overstate their claims: Literacy does not "automatically" cause anything. All the Mountain City women were literate before they came to Al-Anon, but literacy by itself did not bring them what is promised by either the narrative of cognition or the narrative of liberation: There is no literacy standing apart from context that can make us smart or free. Only in a context where personal freedom, spiritual growth, and self-examination were valued and nurtured did the Al-Anon women acquire those attributes, with help from their literacy. My study shows, as does Sylvia Scribner and Michael Cole's research among the Vai, that the qualities acquired with literacy are specific to the uses of literacy. Literacy doesn't cause; it enables.

This work suggests that the enabling qualities of literacy come to the fore most easily when accompanied by dialogue—talking and listening, sharing and supporting. This is the *I-thou* relationship between teacher and learner that I identify in Paula Freire's pedagogy ("Narratives of Literacy"). This is the mutual empathy Jean Baker Miller and Irene Pierce Stiver discuss in *The Healing Connection*. As Lilly says, "If nobody's listened, then you won't speak." The need to be listened to, given permission to speak, may be greater with people from backgrounds of powerlessness, those who have been silenced or marginalized.

This study suggests the interdependence of talk and text. The Al-Anon women emphasized again and again the necessity of conversation. If we look at only what is printed in Al-Anon books and pamphlets without hearing what is said in meetings and between members, we are likely to have a distorted picture. The notion that a written text can be abstracted from its context—from its material and intellectual surroundings, from the lore that goes with it, from the oral tradition that it comes from, and from other related texts— does not seen to jibe with how actual people read or write. Although some academics profess that a text stands alone, no one, not even the most hidebound New Critic, actually uses a text stripped from its context. The meaning of the text depends on its context and its readers, who come to the text with hopes, fears, biases, and knowledge. For the Mountain City women, the oral teachings of the program serve as hermeneutic and corrective for what they read and as prompts and heuristics for what they write.

The texts the Mountain City women read and write are embedded in the rich and caring conversations that go on among the women. Through these conversations, employing the specialized language of the program, the women attain membership in the Al-Anon discourse community. In the case of the Mountain City women, then, orality and literacy are not dichotomous, as Walter Ong posits in *Orality and Literacy* (37–50), but complementary and supplementary. Among the Mountain City Al-Anon women, the relationship between the two communication modes, written and spoken, is far more complex and more interactive than great leap or great divide theories present it, far more like the explanation Shirley Brice Heath gives in her article "Protean Shapes in Literacy Events: Ever-Shifting Oral and Literate Traditions."

Here, Heath argues that it is more useful to regard orality and literacy not as a dichotomy or as a single continuum but as two continua, two traditions, that meet, intersect, and cross in specific human situations (112). Heath concludes that the notion of a single continuum or simple dichotomy omits such important factors as the functions and uses of the discourse, the situation in which the discourse occurs, the cultural norms for the construction of discourse, and the personal motives of speaker or writer. This list comprises a pretty fair definition of the term *rhetoric*. In other words, both orality and literacy—not just orality, as Ong seems to imply—are always already rhetorical: In both modes, people use words to influence others (and themselves) and to draw others into socially cohesive units. Through language—written, read, and spoken—the Al-Anon women negotiate their identities, knowing that self is not an essential unchanging "little me," to use Robert Brooke's expression (15), but rather a fluid entity, sensitive to external conditions and historical constraints and consciously changeable. The self, it seems, is also a rhetorical construct.

Research

It is in this sense of rhetoric that I see the implications of my work for research. Let me explain: In an article called "Composition Studies: Postmodern or Popular," which I have quoted earlier, John Trimbur argues that the task of researchers and teachers in composition should be "to connect rhetoric both to sign systems and to lived experience in order to understand the 'logic of combination' by which individuals splice together a sense of self from the textual shards of the most mass-mediated culture in human history" (130). I hope that my study, even with its limitations and flaws, can stand as an example of this sort of research. Focusing on the popular and the particular, I found, as Trimbur says we will, human agency. By recognizing the agency of ordinary people, we combat the pervasive cynicism of postmodernism, Trimbur explains: He believes that we need to "see how individuals and groups engage in self-formation not as an autonomous activity but as a practice of everyday life, of poaching on the dominant culture to create popular spaces of resistance, evasion, and making do" (130–31).

The women who talked to me practice everyday life using both spoken and written language in a conscious attempt to re-form their experience and their sense of self. They use the master's tools to create space for themselves. With Al-Anon as an important sponsor of their literacy, the Mountain City women resist and evade at least some of the traditional limiting roles allowed to women and have a hand in designing new roles for themselves. They become agents in their own lives. But unless we pay attention to the context and listen to the rhetoric embedded in their literate practices, we are liable to miss the significance of the cultural work these women are doing by means of their literacy.

Similar cultural work, I am convinced, goes on all around us and is open to examination. We have much to learn about literacy from seeing how actual people use it—from, that is, "gaz[ing] in wonderment at the diversity of discursive [and literate] species," to paraphrase Jean-François Lyotard (26). This is in fact the argument that Anne Gere makes in "Kitchen Tables and Rented Rooms." First surveying a number of sites where people outside the academy gather to write, Gere asserts "the need to uncouple literacy and schooling . . . to consider the situatedness of composition practices, to focus on the experiences of writers not always visible to us inside the walls of the academy" (80). When we do so, Gere says, we "take a wider view of composition," avoiding "an uncritical narrative of professionalization" (86) that writes the history of writing instruction using only composition textbooks, university syllabi, and academic journals (78). Research into the "extracurriculum" can reveal not just the gatekeeping function of literacy, Gere argues, but its transformative qualities as well.

Another point about literacy research comes from Brian Street in *Social Literacies: Critical Approaches to Literacy in Development,*

Ethnography, and Education. Despite Street's recognition of the role imagination plays in the human sciences, he offers warnings about the dangers of Ong's "if I were a horse" method to researchers tempted to make pronouncements about the minds of people not available for questioning (155). Of course, we need to think about literacy, but we also need to find confirmation of our ideas in the lives of actual, not theoretical or imaginary, people. When we know more about how literacy works in the lives of actual people in various groups, our theories will be better. When we have more understanding of the vernacular literacies David Barton and Mary Hamilton describe and theorize, we will also be able to formulate a different set of research questions.

Inquiring into the uses and functions of literacies in the lives and work of people outside the academy might also help us study more effectively the literate practices of our students. According to Richard Haswell, the field needs more and better empirical studies of writing. On the Writing-Program Administrators' listserv, Haswell has argued:

> The current state of serious inquiry into rhet/comp is still highly fragmented, most of it is yet so minimal that it has been unable to build up a substantial and incremental and therefore meaningful body of studies and findings, and most of it is largely disregarded by the comp/rhet discipline. And one of the main reasons for this situation is how much the discipline itself is so severely tied to or circumscribed by WPA work.

As an example, Haswell cites a recent collection about scholarship and publication in composition studies, which, he maintains, is more about promotion than about scholarship: "No one [of the writers included] insists that scholarship and publication should be dedicated to a serious search for truths that have a potential to better society." Haswell's solution includes "extend[ing] our concept of the discipline beyond the classroom and embrac[ing] the world." Of course I agree. But I also argue, as modesty prevents Haswell from doing, that his *Gaining Ground in College Writing* is a fairly lonely example of research that supports compositionists' contention that what we do really does improve student writing. Freed by recent theorizing from naive and positivistic notions of research and truth, we ought to undertake empirical studies of writing and of literacy. The more we know about writing, about literate practices, and about oral discursive practices among actual writers and readers, both inside and outside the academy, the better work we will be able to do at both the theoretical and practical levels.

Examples of this sort of inquiry include two recent longitudinal research projects in composition, one by Anne J. Herrington and Marcia Curtis at University of Massachusetts at Amherst and the other by Nancy Sommers at Harvard. Herrington and Curtis's work shows that no matter what we think students are doing with writing assignments across the curriculum, they are sometimes using that writing to clarify their own values, work through their own problems, and define their own identities. Herrington and Curtis's subjects used their literacy for the same thing my Mountain City women did—for their personal development—but the texts those students created are quite different from the writing of the Al-Anon women. Sommers's study of the writing of one class at Harvard over the students' four-year college experience is yielding exciting data about the development of writing at the undergraduate level. In a recent CCCC paper, Sommers argues that even a highly academic, scientific paper can be still personally meaningful work for a student, can be part of her identity formation, can mark for that student important steps in his personal development.

We need to pay special attention to the literate practices of women and girls. I am thinking here of work like Janice Radway's *Reading the Romance,* Jennifer Horsman's *Something in My Mind Besides the Everyday,* and Gere's *Intimate Practices* but also of Meredith Cherland's *Private Practices: Girls Reading Fiction and Constructing Identity,* Margaret Finders's *Just Girls: Hidden Literacies and Life in Junior High,* and Mary Trachsel's "Horse Stories and Romance Fiction: Variants or Alternative Texts of Female Identity," to name only a few. It is true that in the last twenty-five years, the academy—or at least some parts of it—has made serious attempts to examine the experiences of women and girls, but we have a long way to go before the meaning-making activities of women and girls are valued by the culture. What is not valued is not studied. What is not studied is not valued. As a field, composition needs to know what women, at different ages and in different situations, read and write and how they talk about these texts. We begin with inquiry, with collecting data, stories, and texts. In discussing feminist research in composition studies, Gesa Kirsch and Joy Ritchie argue that "theorizing begins with the material, not transcending the personal, but claiming it" (7). Doing so, composition research can "become a location for reconsidering what counts as knowledge," they argue (8). While I am somewhat less optimistic, I do assert that opportunities for research into the literate practices of women abound.

Readers will understand, I hope, that I am not urging the renunciation of theory for inquiry. In the past, composition studies suffered from the lack of theory, and I have argued elsewhere that theory is not only necessary but desirable ("Theory, Theory Talk, and Composition"). As a field, we have profited immensely from the theoretical speculation of the last few years. It has made us smarter, more critical of received knowledge. But theory without inquiry leads to paralysis, as both Dorothy Smith and Trimbur assert in their respective critiques of postmodernism. Theory is a tool box, Michel Foucault and Gilles Deleuze say, a way to look from specific practices outward (208). I hope that my small study shows that starting with specific practices is possible.

Pedagogy

The most important implication of my research for pedagogy, I believe, lies in the powerful combination of reading and writing and talk. Most composition teachers already know this, of course. What I have observed from the Mountain City women and from my own teaching is that when people are engaged in genuine discussion—which cannot be generated by fill-in-the-blank- or guess-what's-in-the-professor's-mind questions—they find their related reading and writing personally meaningful. Even though this insight is nothing new, some elaboration may help.

For the Mountain City women, reading, writing, and talk are integrated into the rich mix of their relationships. In contrast, school, an early and formative sponsor of literacy, often presents reading and writing as solitary, isolated, and isolating activities, the purpose of which, all too often, eludes students. Jen reminds us in chapter 2 that school-sponsored writing was something that had had little meaning for her; about her first Fourth Step, she says, "It was like an English theme. I felt like I was doing an assignment for English class. I could not see any connection between what I was doing and what it was supposed to result in. So to me it wasn't helpful, but it was helpful to my sponsor." This is not, unfortunately, an uncommon view of writing: that papers written for class have no personal purpose.

Often focusing on forms at the sentence or genre level, school writing is *for* someone else, not a way for a person to work out meaning for herself. But after years of writing for her own purposes in Al-Anon, Jennifer learned that the writing she did in her graduate classes, while still partly writing *for* someone else, was now also *for* her, too. When she was finally able to integrate her own experiences with her academic reading and express her own view of the concepts, she was surprised: "This is not normally what I'd put in a class paper." Teachers can, I believe, foster a sense among students that when they write for *us*, they are also making meaning for themselves; this is of course something we try to do in first-year classes but our success varies. When we "uncouple" literacy from schooling, as I have tried to do with this work, it becomes easier to see what motivates people to write and what purposes people have for writing when they are not compelled to. One of those purposes, my study shows, is to be part of a group striving for a common goal. Establishing a college class as such a group is easier said than done, but the composition literature is full of success stories.

The critique of school-sponsored literacy implied by my study extends as well to reading. As we saw in chapter 3, the Mountain

City women certainly read efferently, for information, but they prefer to read aesthetically, for the experience of reading. I argue that a large part of that experience is the conversation that goes on around the texts. Grappling with material in concert with others, the women learn to apply nonfiction texts to their lives. In addition, the Mountain City women talk with animation about the fiction they read. They become emotionally involved. They do not see the purpose of reading as the dissection of novels or plays in order to locate text features, which then indicate meaning.

For example, when asked about *Beloved,* Lilly seemed reluctant, readers may recall, to offer an assertion of its (one) meaning, to talk about it in a literary way:

> I don't think I understood it all, not intellectually. But all my feelings got it. It touched every feeling I'd ever had. . . .
> I understood that book in terms of my feelings. But in terms of how it all fits together on an intellectual level, if I had to analyze it, I'd be a little lost.

I wonder now whether the question I asked about *Beloved* sounded too much like an English professor's question. What I've learned is that starting with feelings, with the reader's response to a text, also works in my classroom. The Mountain City women prefer to read aesthetically—that is, for the experience—rather than efferently—that is, for information only. Perhaps instructors need to pay more attention to the aesthetic, experiential end of the continuum, rather than focusing all our energies on the efferent, informational end.

As someone who has devoted her life to teaching English, I found most distressing Lilly's comment that

> I've realized that reading is an intense pleasure. You can learn from it. It can be painful. It can be all kinds of things. But I always thought reading had to do with school and learning. It was not a fun thing. It was not a soothing thing. That, in recovery, has just blossomed.

These negative remarks are not uncommon responses to school reading, as we know from our students. The question is, Who is teaching students that reading is not a "fun thing"? Am *I* doing this? Why are we *not* teaching them that reading can be soothing? Why are we *not* helping students learn that reading can be the "intense pleasure" Lilly describes?

One reason, of course, is that for students, reading in school is work, and anything labeled work is less pleasurable than something classed as leisure. I understand that. I understand the usual television excuse as well. But I also understand that English teachers—at all levels—sometimes impose alienation from literary texts on young people. We demand thesis statements summarizing the meanings of the texts. We focus on details of plot. We count off when they don't know the names of the minor characters. We disparage their emotional responses. In fact, we privilege texts. We are trained to do this. Here's an example:

For my sabbatical lecture, I read the last half of chapter 3, the sections about the Mountain City women reading fiction and poetry. The questions from my colleagues afterward focused almost entirely on the literary texts I'd mentioned. My colleagues talked about the texts as genres and about the meaning of the genres and the reasons those genres would appeal to my research participants; they made interesting connections between characters in the novels; they said very smart things about mysteries and the recent fiction of African American women writers. My audience offered helpful suggestions on how I might "recover" the texts that had been "lost" in the Mountain City women's discussion. But their point was the texts while mine was the readers. The Mountain City women who talked to me *use* books to form community, to come to an understanding of their own worth, to examine the moral questions they face in their lives, to see how other people act and survive in times of adversity, to stimulate desire and extend the range of the possible. For them, books are "equipment for living," not art objects. What the Mountain City women learned about "little murders" in relationships is, I contend, far more valuable than any assessment of the literary merit of Alice Walker's novel. What is important, I believe, is the meaning the *readers* make from texts.

Of course, some of my colleagues understand this. Lee Morrissey, who teaches seventeenth- and eighteenth-century literature, organizes his courses on the question of literacy. Citing theological texts and political pamphlets, the Civil War, and especially the killing of the king, Morrissey points out the dangers of writing and reading: This is what can happen when ordinary people are allowed to write and read, to create their own meanings. And so, according to Morrissey, the purpose of criticism since its beginnings in the eighteenth century has been to govern reading, to tame its power by setting a class of experts between the text and reader. Is it possible to give reading back so that, like the clubwomen Gere writes about or the women who talked to me, ordinary people are allowed to make their own meaning from texts?

Another implication for pedagogy may be found in the conversation among the Mountain City women that goes on around the texts. Recall Lilly's comment about reading Ntozake Shange's *for colored girls:* "I loved watching what people liked. The more conversation we added about it, the fuller everything got, because there were so many different ways to look at one poem, depending on who felt what from it." Perhaps we need the reminder that, no matter how many times we've studied or taught a text, there is no one right answer. In chapter 3, I discussed Gere's comments about how turn-of-the-century literature textbooks allowed for no personal response, reinforcing the notion that the text has *a* meaning, which readers must be told by an authority or find in isolation. The literacy of the clubwomen subverted this, allowing meaning to be multiple and communal. As Michael Holzman once wrote: "Only in school are people who fail to decode a text not helped by those around them" (30). Why not? We can, I believe, use conversation to help our students see the richness of a text, the variety of meanings a text can have.

In fact, according to Kevin Dettmar, a good text is not required in order to have this kind of class discussion. In an MLA presentation on the canon in Joyce's *Portrait of the Artist,* Dettmar says,

> Unfortunately, we can't ensure good conversations with texts simply by canonizing them. . . . Likewise, we can't prevent—and surely, shouldn't try to prevent—good readers from having complex and rewarding conversations with nearly worthless texts (this is one of the important lessons of cultural studies).

Dettmar speaks here from experience, using current movies—not "film"—and rock lyrics to explore the concept of irony.

I, on the other hand, would certainly claim that the texts I teach in my rhetoric classes are "good" ones, even canonical ones. At the end of each semester, I ask my students to write an assessment of their response papers, including not only what they learned from writing about the assigned readings but also what they learned from the responses of their peers. They write in specific ways about how one or another student helped them learn both what rhetoric is and how to read the often difficult texts in the course. Sounding a little like Lilly, they talk about how the various responses from their peers make the rhetorical concepts richer and their own understanding more sophisticated. They learn, as well, that they contribute to the conversation. Yes, my students do sometimes miss out on the wonderful things I know about Plato, Aristotle, Burke, or Perelman. But long ago I decided that what they learn by presenting their own readings and listening to their peers is more valuable than the things I don't get to say. For they learn from experience, as do the Mountain City Al-Anon women, that they *can* read and write and influence others by doing so.

The point here seems to me to be that the ideology of school writing and reading has too often left the student as human being out of the formula. When the goal is to transfer information efficiently, as it so often is in American schooling, writing becomes forms, and reading becomes the right answers. Perhaps the link between expressive writing and aesthetic reading is that in both, the person, the student, is important. What the person experiences is the purpose. I am not arguing for an emphasis on students' emotions over their intellectual activity. From time to time, I have to remind students that the point of the response papers is not to vent or effuse, though they can start there, but to wrestle with the ideas. Knowledge, ideas, texts are not and should not be disembodied entities, divorced from students'—or other people's—selves.

At this point, I wish to issue a strong caveat. I am not advocating spiritual or therapeutic writing techniques for the classroom. Therapeutic writing may and perhaps should go on outside the academy—in the extracurriculum, as one practice of vernacular literacy—with consenting adults. For those interested in such writing, I suggest the self-help section of Barnes and Noble, where a number of books on journaling and freewriting for personal growth or for healing from trauma can be found. The role of emotion or of spirituality, loosely defined, in writing has recently been explored in three collections for composition studies, Regina Foehr and Susan Schiller's *The Spiritual Side of Writing*, Alice Glarden Brand and Richard Graves's *Presence of Mind· Writing and the Domain Beyond the Cognitive*, and Charles Anderson and Marian MacCurdy's *Writing and Healing*. These books remind us of the rich possibilities of writing, but none recommends irresponsible pedagogy.

And it is irresponsible for English instructors to set out to intervene in their students' psyches. Most of us are, whether we like it or not, agents of the state, as Jim Berlin used to point out, and as such need to exercise caution inquiring into our students' private lives. More importantly, we are not trained to intervene. The women in my study were all adults. Not all our students are. The Mountain City women went to Al-Anon on their own and then chose to submit themselves to its spiritual practice. In our classes, students cannot make those choices freely. They have to do what we say. Being neither priests nor psychologists, we need to be careful not to assign true-confession papers rather than personal narrative—and there is a difference. Personal-narrative papers ask students to connect ideas to their lived or observed experience. True-confession assignments explicitly ask students to reveal private moments. Personal narrative papers ask students to narrate in a logical form their lived or observed experience and then to analyze, to reflect on, to question, and to interpret what happened. True-confession papers ask them simply to narrate or to recount feelings. True-confession papers are what James Pennebaker asked his subjects to write about in his psychological experiments, but he had consent forms, and the students were free to leave at any time—what they wrote did not count for a grade.

But even when we don't solicit stories of personal trauma, we get them. What do we do about the troubled young people who attend our classes? When we see in a student text or in conference or in class discussion a student struggling with personal problems, as we all do from time to time, we show concern, we treat the student as if he or she is more important than the assignment or the grade, and, when appropriate, we make the proper referrals, even walking the student to the counseling center if necessary. We do not hold criminal or dangerous activity as confidential. We behave as caring adults, bearing some responsibility, but not all, for the human beings around us. We realize we teach in a society where students often need someone, anyone, to listen to their stories, as Dan Morgan explains in his thoughtful article "Ethical Issues Raised by Students' Personal Writing."

Of course, all teachers should be sensitive to the wounds students sometimes carry and be respectful of their religious and spiritual lives. This last does not include *not* challenging students' beliefs, but it does mean doing so with an understanding of the differences that exist among spirituality, religion, and ideology. It never hurts students to learn that other people don't believe the same way they do; isn't that what college is for? But teachers do need to recognize that for some people the profoundest part of their identity is their religious beliefs or spiritual life. Despite the separation of church and state, religion, for many people, is not a hobby (see chapter 2, particularly, of Stephen Carter's *The Culture of Disbelief*), and so we must treat these beliefs with respect.

Carrying the Message to Others: Voice and Self

Like literary criticism, school is a way of governing meaning, a way for the culture to control its members. This is not altogether a bad thing. Indeed, there is no literacy without context, no reading free from constraints, no writing emancipated from conventions. The reading and writing of the women who talked with me were guided by Al-Anon, by its talk and its texts, and by the standards of the particular Al-Anon community in Mountain City. It is therefore well for those of us who teach not to be seduced by romantic visions of what we can achieve in school, a place whose ideological function and institutional character mitigate against the kind of transformative power that both literacy and spirituality can offer. But sometimes, by being subversive, we can "restore discourse to its character as an event," as Foucault puts it in "The Order of Discourse" (1164). Sometimes we can show that what Foucault calls "true discourse" occurs not in what discourse says but in what discourse is or what it does (1156). As individuals we cannot change the ordering of discourse permanently, but we can look for those times when something happens, when something changes, as we use language.

It is in this sort of event, I maintain, where the transformative power of literacy is to be found. In his Afterword to Lyotard's *The Postmodern Explained,* Wlad Godzich seems to concur. Like many twentieth-century thinkers, Godzich unfortunately begins his theoretical discussion of reading with speculation about the Greeks' early literacy, which he treats as axiomatic. (Once again, I contend that despite the rhetoric of Havelock and Ong, the psychological processes of the ancient Greeks as they read, three millennia ago, are not something we can know.) This problem aside, Godzich nonetheless offers a postmodern view of literacy and self that, I think, can apply. Reading words aloud, words that don't "belong" to anyone because they are already there, a reader experiences "an intrusion," Godzich says, which "precipitates a sudden awareness of the self" (132). Reading then "actually constitutes us as subjects, for reading enacts our relation to something that is outside us," Godzich explains (132–33). Here the text is "other," the whetstone against which we struggle, as Stanley Fish says, to find virtue or meaning. I would add that reading—and writing—do not automatically constitute us as subjects but can if the context allows it. The context of the Mountain City Al-Anon women teaches them explicitly that their reading and their writing can be self-constituting activities.

According to Godzich, Lyotard believes that "the central problem of postmodernity is indeed that of our ability to read, the problem of literacy, not in E. D. Hirsch, Jr.'s sense or that of the advocates of so-called functional literacy, but in the subject-constituting sense" (134). Godzich explains that modern reading, as distinguished from the postmodern kind, assumes

> the existence of a freestanding subject who must be equipped with the know-how to engage in a suitable technology of knowledge appropriation so that he or she may acquire knowledge, use it, transform it, and then exchange it. It is a literacy in the service of an apparatus of knowledge. . . . Children who are taught this sort of literacy become the servants of this knowledge apparatus. They are constituted by it as subjects, to be sure, but in the sense of being subjected to it. (135)

Clearly this happens with "modern" writing, too; students learn to write in the service of a knowledge apparatus and produce texts they never expect to find personally meaningful. According to Godzich, "Lyotard's notion of reading . . . advocates a relentless relearning of reading, a reiteration of this constitutive moment" (135). What Lyotard envisions is not literacy as gatekeeper but as event, literacy as transforming, literacy making one aware of self in relation to other selves. This is the kind of literacy the Mountain City women tell us about. But this sort of literacy doesn't just happen; it has to be nurtured.

The Lyotard-Godzich view of reading is useful in helping us understand the relation of literacy and self. Yet, it is important, I think, to note that Godzich continues to treat the subject as individuated, separate, apart from others, as Smith claims is common in post-modernist-poststructuralist thought. Smith argues persuasively that even though the existence of the subject as a unified whole is denied in postmodernism, the knowing subject is spoken of as a singular consciousness, separate from others. As we have seen, the self-formation of the Mountain City women is social. The social experience of literacy, I argue, not the literacy itself, constitutes these selves. The literacy that Gere presents in her study of the club-women ("Common Properties") and that I see with my students (when my pedagogy works) is not individual but rather communal, social, like the socially constructed subjects and objects Smith describes in her defense of research after postmodernism. There is no denying, of course, that "we all walk around inside our own skins," as Dianne Schallert used to say to her psycholinguistics classes at Texas. But the formation of self, like Vygotsky's formation of thought, is social in origin.

In the social, communal literacy of the Mountain City Al-Anon women, human beings join with one another and with texts in a communion of friendship to come to voice and self: "Teaching how to write and how to read is also teaching voice and self" (Swearingen 234).

Appendixes

References

Index

Appendix A: The Twelve Steps of Al-Anon

1. We admitted we were powerless over alcohol—that our lives had become unmanageable.
2. Came to believe that a Power greater than ourselves could restore us to sanity.
3. Made a decision to turn our will and our lives over to the care of God *as we understood Him.*
4. Made a searching and fearless moral inventory of ourselves.
5. Admitted to God, to ourselves, and to another human being the exact nature of our wrongs.
6. Were entirely ready to have God remove all these defects of character.
7. Humbly asked Him to remove our shortcomings.
8. Made a list of all persons we had harmed and became willing to make amends to them all.
9. Made direct amends to such people wherever possible except when to do so would injure them or others.
10. Continued to take personal inventory and when we were wrong promptly admitted it.
11. Sought through prayer and meditation to improve our conscious contact with God *as we understood Him,* praying only for knowledge of His will for us and the power to carry that out.
12. Having had a spiritual awakening as the result of these Steps, we tried to carry this message to others, and to practice these principles in all our affairs.

The Twelve Steps of Al-Anon, as adapted by Al-Anon with permission of Alcoholics Anonymous World Services, Inc. (A.A.W.S.), are reprinted with permission of Al-Anon and A.A.W.S. A.A.W.S.'s permission to reprint the material does not mean the A.A.W.S. has reviewed or approved the contents of this publication or that A.A.W.S. necessarily agrees with the views expressed therein. Alcoholics Anonymous is a program of recovery from alcoholism *only*—use or permissible adaptation of A.A.'s Twelve Steps in connection with programs and activities which are patterned after A.A., but which address other problems, or in any other non-A.A. context, does not imply otherwise. Although Alcoholics Anonymous is a spiritual program, A.A. is not a religious program, and use of A.A. material in the present connection does not imply A.A.'s affiliation with or endorsement of any sect, denomination, or specific religious belief.

Appendix B: An Essay on Research and Telling the Truth

In chapter 1, "A Dais for My Words," I talked about how I did the research for this project, but I fear I made it sound too easy. In this essay, I share my thoughts on the difficulties of writing about interview research. I talk about practical and ethical problems I encountered. Along the way, I discuss such mundane things as pronouns and such lofty topics as rhetoric and truth in a postmodern age. I hope that what I say here can serve as a contribution for further discussion, in composition and rhetoric, of the responsibilities of research.

About Writing the Research

The problem isn't, as research courses had led me to believe, doing research with human subjects but writing it. When I began, I thought it would be quick and easy: go ask the women questions about reading, writing, spirituality, and power; take good notes; then write up what they say. But in writing, I encountered at least three practical and ethical problems in translating my interview research data into a text that tells the truth. And that word *truth*, trailing as it does clouds of positivism, is the issue in all the problems.

In my rhetoric classes, I teach that what we call truth, what we know, is belief socially justified by particular uses and forms of language, which are contingent and communal, not permanent or individual. At the same time, all the communities I identify with not only value telling the truth, however that truth is arrived at, but also hold individuals responsible for telling it. While no single immutable truth exists out there somewhere about the relationship of literacy and spirituality, what I write must be true, I believe, if I am to offer it as new knowledge.

In composition studies, however, what counts or should count as knowledge and what counts as appropriate data and warrants have not, for a variety of reasons, been totally settled. Speaking out of this methodological mix, Linda Brodkey ("Writing") and Thomas Newkirk explain that case study research like my project is not lower-order empirical research, as it is often purported to be (see, for example, MacNealy 195), but rather another route to knowledge. According to Brodkey, "We study other people's stories not because they are true or even because they are false, but for the same reason that people tell and listen to them, in order to learn about the terms on which others make sense of their lives" ("Writing" 47). This view assumes that learning from the lived experience of others is possible.

Nonetheless, both Newkirk and Brodkey are clear that it is not the case study method but rather the case study *researcher* telling the stories of the experiences of others. According to Newkirk, case study researchers tell "transformative narratives, ones in which the individual experiences some sort of conflict and undergoes a qualitative change in the resolution of that conflict" (134). What makes case studies work, he says, is the "cultural myths" or "mythic narratives" (135, 136) that researchers use as warrants in order to make the move from "empirically collected data" (Brodkey, "Writing" 26)—that is to say, from the responses elicited by the surveys and answers brought forth by interview questions—to the stories "not yet heard" by the academy (Brodkey, "Writing" 48). All this makes perfect sense to me—and fits my agenda. For, to tell the truth, I want to tell a particular transformation story about the role reading and writing can take in personal and spiritual development. But I am troubled, nonetheless, by the implication that the story is the researcher's or the culture's but not necessarily the research participants'.

This runs me smack into what Michel Foucault, in "The Order of Discourse," calls the will to truth. Included in Foucault's list of procedures for controlling discourse is the opposition between true and false, which requires that we dismiss what is labeled false and keep what counts as true (1155–57). According to Foucault, since at least the time of Plato, Western culture has sought the truth in the relation of utterance to referent (1156). Twenty-five hundred years later, the word *truth* still means a match between words and things. In the academy, *truth* continues to carry the weight of empirical, controlled experiments manipulating some part of nature to get at what's really out there: Truth is external to us, and if we observe carefully using the right instruments, we can find it, and if we are careful reporters, eschewing the figures of rhetoric, we can convey it (see Bazerman for an account of how this deeply held assumption came to be). Of course, we postmodernists know that the relation between words and things is always tenuous. We understand that central to all research is interpretation, as Peter Mortensen and Gesa Kirsch say: The researcher's "values permeate and shape the research questions, observations, and conclusions" (xxi). We are aware that research like mine is not replicable in a positivistic sense. Yet, what I write must be somehow true to the empirically collected data, that is, to the tapes of the interviews and to the 161 transcript pages of the women's responses. What I write, I believe, must reflect what the Mountain City Al-Anon women said in answer to the questions I asked. The story I tell must be not just mine or the culture's but also my research participants'. Writing the truth about this research is more complicated than I had thought it would be.

About the Number of Research Participants

In writing a narrative that would meet all these constraints and at the same time be readable, I have encountered several truth problems (for elaboration, see my article "The Will to Truth"). The first was the number of participants. In the summers of 1990 and 1991, I actually interviewed six women, one other besides Tommie, Jennifer, Judy, Jill, and Catherine. Later, I included Lilly. Yet, from the first, I worried about one of the original research participants, the one unnamed. The stories of her life that she told in the first interview were troubling. Some of her responses had little relation to my questions. In the follow-up interview during the second summer, when I sought verification of what had been said in the first summer, her responses were inconsistent. From what she was now telling me about her life, I began to understand that she was under great stress.

The question was whether to include what she said or leave it out. My ambivalence shows up in the early conference papers I wrote about this project. In some, I say I have five research participants, in others six, and in still others seven. When I started to write this book, I had to decide whether to include this woman, even peripherally. In the end, my decision came from considering how I *felt* about presenting her publicly. It felt like betraying a trust. In the prologue to his memoir *All Over but the Shoutin'*, journalist Rick Bragg says, "The errors in this book that I know of are omissions, not fabrications, intended to spare people who have enough pain in their lives, a little more" (xxi). I do not know that including this woman's responses in my published work would cause her pain, but I decided I was not willing to take the chance.

About Positionality

A second truth problem was this: Beyond explaining the relationships between me and the women who volunteered to be interviewed for my project, how much of my own life do I need to reveal? To share in print secrets that are not mine alone might be hurtful to others. Besides, still haunted by the specter of the research tradition, I don't want this book to be about me, although I know that it is and can't help being. I want *A Communion of Friendship* to be, rather, about the Mountain City Al-Anon women who use literacy to get better, who use texts, their own as well as other people's, to create a spiritual perspective and a spiritual community. I want what I write to be a corrective to the sometimes reductionist ways academics have talked about literacy: transferring information, restructuring the mind, improving one's economic status, exhibiting or claiming power over others, sorting people into categories and then making judgments about them. I want to challenge a tradition that has historically been dismissive not only of the lived experiences of ordinary women (variations of feminism notwithstanding) but also of the emotional and the spiritual as legitimate categories for academic discussions of reading and writing (but see articles by Berthoff and coauthors; Foehr and Schiller; Anderson and MacCurdy).

But surely readers need to know something about the lenses I see through. Does that include more details of my life than I've already revealed? Readers may find it helpful to know that my terministic screens are rhetorical, feminist, Marxist, therapeutic, and spiritual (of the Twelve-Step and Episcopal varieties). Readers may assume that when one of the Mountain City women is irreverent or uses risque language, she knows that I will not be offended—that I have probably spoken similarly in that same conversation. Readers may assume, as well, that when a participant talks about her spiritual experiences, she knows that that is a subject I, too, take seriously, though my definition of particular terms may and probably do differ. Borrowing from Mortensen and Kirsch, I want to "reveal . . . my positionality" but not cross "the thin line" into "self-centered display" (xxvii).

About Ellipsis, Arrangement, Pronouns, and Brackets

The third truth problem started out as surface language concerns. As I wrote, I gathered sections of discourse on the same topic from different parts of an interview and spliced those sections together. For example, Lilly talks about reading mystery novels all through her interview, not just when I asked her specifically about reading mystery novels, so I juxtapose a comment from the beginning of her interview with something she said near the end. When I do this, I use ellipses to show that I have omitted intervening material. Sometimes, there are so many ellipses that reading the passage is difficult, so I leave them all out, even though their absence indicates a smooth, continuous flow of words that did not occur in the interview. I worry that I am distorting—even though the passage I've put together seems to me to be faithful to the speaker's ideas and feelings.

Sometimes in working with a passage, I consider what I called in graduate school Maxine's Dictum—according to Professor Hairston,

"If a reader can get lost, the reader will get lost"—and move a sentence from the middle of a chunk of language to the beginning so that readers will know what the topic is. Sometimes, I move a sentence to the end of a quotation so that readers will see a research participant's current position or conclusion. When I rearrange, am I telling the truth? If so, how much of this am I allowed to do?

A similar situation occurs with the pronouns. The women who talked to me go on for many transcript pages about *it*. The antecedent is in my question, which I have usually not included in the manuscript, or the antecedent is implied in the research participant's narrative, or it's a belief or value she and I share. I know what *it* means because I asked the question, because I've listened to the tape, because I have the transcript right in front of me, because I have been a participant in the community, because I know the woman who was talking. Sometimes I put the antecedent in square brackets following the pronoun, sometimes I put the antecedent in square brackets and leave out the pronoun, and sometimes I just put the antecedent in instead of the pronoun and without brackets. Like the ellipses, the brackets are sometimes so intrusive that they interfere with the reading. Do my readers need the imprecision that I, focusing on coherence, am trying to erase?

It has been my intention to offer an accurate rendition of what the Mountain City women said, but merely attempting to make the text organized and readable distorts. Perhaps this, rather than encouragement to deceive and manipulate, is what Gorgias meant in the fourth-century B.C.E. when he said, "All who have and do persuade people of things do so by molding a false argument" (52). If you tell it so that it is comprehensible and therefore believable, you have already distorted.

About Research and Telling the Truth

As a writer who aims to be understood and as a researcher who wants to be accurate, I am torn. Am I putting words in their mouths? Am I telling the truth? Is there a truth that exists between the certitude —the "hard standards of reliability, validity, and generalizability"—

of positivism, on the one hand, and the abstract, theoretical, and sometimes paralyzing relativism of postmodernism, with its emphasis on representation and contingency, on the other (Mortensen and Kirsch xxi)?

What exists between these two extremes is argument, according to Chaim Perelman. In *The New Rhetoric*, Perelman and Lucie Olbrechts-Tyteca define the problem of Western epistemology as dualism, binaries "of knowledge and opinion, of irrefutable self-evidence and deceptive will, of a universally accepted objectivity and incommunicable subjectivity, of a reality binding on everybody and values that are purely individual" (510). We can add to this list the certitude of positivism and the relativism of postmodernism. In *The Realm of Rhetoric*, Perelman explains the way out of this impasse: "All intellectual activity which is placed between the necessary and the arbitrary is reasonable only to the degree that it is maintained by arguments and eventually clarified by controversies which normally do not lead to unanimity" (159). So, the truth I tell depends on my rhetorical skills?

Newkirk and Brodkey seem to answer in the affirmative. According to Newkirk, because my research is of the case study variety, the story I present will be convincing only if it retells some cultural myth my readers already believe or want to. That's easy enough: The mythic narrative I tell is perhaps the essential American narrative: people remaking their lives, reinventing themselves. The people in this version do so by using literacy as one of their tools. Literacy is not the only tool and perhaps not even a necessary one, but it is the one I focus on. Unlike the grand narratives, in which literacy is said to bestow certain qualities on human beings, the literacy story I recount here is a little narrative, one that does not claim to be generalizable to other populations (see also MacNealy 195–213) but that does aim to add to our knowledge of "the diversity of discursive [or literate] species" (Lyotard 26). To sum up, I have to tell a story that is familiar enough to be believable. At the same time, it must meet the standards of reason set by my community. Furthermore, the story should offer something new: people or places or situations that the academy has neglected or a view that is different from the standard version of what the academy already knows or assumes.

The problem is that postmodernism denies the possibility of finding new knowledge or of telling any story other than one's own. The impossibility of language being referential or unbiased, the questioning of the researcher's position in regard to the subjects or objects of research, the ethics of representation—all have made inquiry and telling the truth seem hopelessly naive or altogether impossible. Feminist sociologist Dorothy Smith explains in an essay called "Telling the Truth after Postmodernism" that poststructualist-postmodern thought argues against the authority of lived experience because, from this perspective, experience is defined as itself discursively determined. Such a formulation, Smith says, "repudiates the very possibility of discovering what is not already posited. The validity of inquiry as a project is removed" (102). Can we learn from other people's experiences, then, or are we caught in an infinite regress of narration and representation?

Smith begins her answer by critiquing the postmodernist-poststructuralist treatment of the individuated subject:

> Though postmodernism rejects the unitary subject, knowing and knowledge remain functions of an individuated consciousness. Throughout [postmodernist/poststructuralist theory], the individuation of the subject is preserved, whether as fragmented, multiplied, layered, or various. (107)

Smith is right. Thus, while postmodernism allows us "multiple narratives revealing varied and many-sided versions of the world from multiple and fragmented discursively constituted positions" (Smith 101), it omits the truly social from formulations of self and language and consequently from the concepts of research, knowledge, and truth. I have used this point elsewhere in this book to critique both Foucault on confession and Godzich on reading as a subject-constituting activity. Smith goes beyond critique to posit an alternative theory "which does not view 'knowledge' as a solipsism of discourse, but preserves people's active presence and views knowledge as a definite form of social act in which an object world is constituted by participants as a world in common" (109).

Drawing on George Herbert Mead, Mikhail Bakhtin, and Velentin Volosinov as key sources for her alternate theory, Smith argues that meaning, reference, truth occurs *in* the social act: " 'Referring' is a concerting of consciousnesses through symbolic communication that gives presence to an object for participants in the emerging course of a social act" (115). To explain, Smith uses stories from her own experience, from observations of interactions between children and their mothers, from Helen Keller's narrative about learning language, and from Frederick Grinnell's account of teaching biology. In one of these, Smith is watching a little girl of about six pull on her mother's skirt, saying, "A cat, a cat, momma, look, a cat." The mother, engaged in conversation with another adult, ignored her daughter at first but then looked in the direction the child was pointing and, seeing a black cat washing herself, said, "Yes, Karen, a cat!" Immediately the child was satisfied (117). Of this incident Smith says:

> Here (it seemed to me) was a child's practice of the social organization constituting an object *among* participants. The other's look and recognition of the object 'seen' and named by the speaker is made accountable by the mother's 'yes.' 'Cat' is thereby constituted or completed *as object* as the other accountably recognized what the speaker sees. The *social* 'grammar' of naming and identifying or referring to objects called for a missing complement, the other's 'recognition' in her assent, her glance towards the object, and her repetition of 'its' name. Once the mother completed the sequence by registering that she had seen the cat Karen indicated, the sequence was completed to Karen's apparent satisfaction. (117, Smith's emphases)

Smith concludes that "the name-look-recognition sequence among people produces the object world among us and for each other" (118). An object gains its status as real—"that is, an object for others as well as for the speaker" (118)—as this sequence is completed: "Even when the response corrects ['No, Dave, not bird. Fish!'], the object has already been brought into the social act" (119). This same grammar is clear in the other illustrations Smith offers—medical students recognizing cells and cell structure only after they have been introduced to histology, a young friend navigating by matching a map to the actual features of the neighborhood while Smith drove.

Having established the grammar of making objects real, Smith then argues that the same process takes place over longer periods of time and space:

> Scientific techniques and technologies of observation, and systematic note-taking, supplant the immediacy of Karen's cries and pointing to the cat, but they are organized by the same sequential 'grammar.' They are intended to enable other[s] . . . to track and find the object they have introduced into this particular sequence of the social act of science. (124)

Some scientific papers, Smith points out, leave "the achievement of the object at the 'Mommy, there's a cat' stage" (124).

Referring is always problematic, Smith says. The name-look-recognition sequence assumes a second person who can look or who knows how to follow the instructions or understand the demonstration in the text. The possibility always exists that the second person may look and not see the cat. Such a dialogic view of truth or knowledge expects "multiple and divergent perspectives" (130) and allows for the possibility that some inquiry will fail or be modified in the discursive process—"No, Dave, not bird. Fish!"

Smith's dialogic view fleshes out Perelman's theoretical argument about argument: What lies between the arbitrary and the necessary isn't the argument in a person's head; it is the argument presented to the community, where it is challenged and seldom agreed to unanimously or all at once. Smith's view gives substance to Newkirk's and Brodkey's explanations of case study research; it is a valid way of saying "Look, there's a cat," to which readers can say, "Yes, it is a cat, though I've never seen it there before" or "Well, I didn't know cats did that" or "Maybe we should look for more cats like this and study them. Or we could see if dogs do this."

Smith's work counters the postmodernist implication that inquiry into the actual (that is, what lies beyond the text or language) is either an impossibility (because there really isn't anything beyond the language) or an exercise in solipsism (because it really is only about the researcher anyway). Smith allows me and other researchers in composition to study the literate practices of actual people without making positivistic claims or recounting endless autobiography.

A Communion of Friendship is like Karen's "Look, mommy, a cat." The truth I tell depends on whether the community I write for sees the cat or at least takes my observations into account in discussions about the existence or nature of the cat.

References

Al-Anon Family Groups. *Blueprint for Progress: Al-Anon's Fourth-Step Inventory.* New York: Al-Anon, 1976.

———. *Courage to Change: One Day at a Time in Al-Anon II.* New York: Al-Anon, 1992.

———. *In All Our Affairs: Making Crises Work for You.* New York: Al-Anon, 1990.

———. *One Day at a Time in Al-Anon.* 1973. 17th ed. New York: Al-Anon, 1983.

Alcoholics Anonymous World Services. *Alcoholics Anonymous.* 3rd ed. New York: Alcoholics Anonymous, 1976.

Allan, Graham. *Friendship: Developing a Sociological Perspective.* Boulder: Westview, 1989.

Anderson, Charles M., and Marian MacCurdy, eds. *Writing and Healing: Toward an Informed Practice.* Urbana: NCTE, 2000.

Anonymous. "I Came to Believe: Ethnography, Anonymity, and the Private I." *College Composition and Communication* 46 (1995): 282–84.

Aristotle. *On Rhetoric: A Theory of Civic Discourse.* Trans. George A. Kennedy. New York: Oxford UP, 1991.

Baldwin, Christina. *Life's Companion: Journal Writing as a Spiritual Quest.* New York: Bantam, 1990.

Barthes, Roland. *The Pleasure of the Text.* Trans. Richard Miller. New York: Hill, 1975.

Barton, David, and Mary Hamilton. *Local Literacies: Reading and Writing in One Community.* New York: Routledge, 1998.

Bazerman, Charles. "Reporting the Experiment: The Changing Account of Scientific Doings in the Philosophical Transactions of the Royal Society, 1665–1800." *Landmark Essays on Rhetoric of Science.* Ed. Randy Allen Harris. Mahwah, NJ: Hermagoras, 1997. 169–86. Rpt. of chapter 3, *Shaping Written Knowledge: The Genre and Activity of the Experimental Article in Science.* Madison: U of Wisconsin P, 1998.

Berthoff, Ann E. "I. A. Richards and the Concept of Literacy." *The Sense of Learning.* Portsmouth, NH: Boynton/Cook, 1990. 136–49.

Berthoff, Ann E., Beth Daniell, JoAnn Campbell, C. Jan Swearingen, and James Moffett. "Interchanges: Spiritual Sites of Composing." *College Composition and Communication* 45 (1994): 237–63.

Bizzell, Patricia. *Academic Discourse and Critical Consciousness.* Pittsburgh: U of Pittsburgh P, 1992.

Bizzell, Patricia, and Bruce Herzberg. *The Rhetorical Tradition: Readings from Classical Times to the Present*. Boston: Bedford, 1990.

Bragg, Rick. *All Over but the Shoutin'*. New York: Pantheon, 1997.

Brand, Alice Glarden, and Richard L. Graves. *Presence of Mind: Writing and the Domain Beyond the Cognitive*. Portsmouth, NH: Boynton/Cook, 1994.

Brandt, Deborah. "Accumulating Literacy: Writing and Learning to Write in the Twentieth Century." *College English* 57 (1995): 649–68.

——. "Remembering Writing, Remembering Reading." *College Composition and Communication* 45 (1994): 459–79.

——. "Sponsors of Literacy." *College Composition and Communication* 49 (1998): 165–85.

Brodkey, Linda. "On the Subject of Class and Gender in 'The Literacy Letters.'" *College English* 51 (1989): 125–41.

——. "Writing Ethnographic Narratives." *Written Communication* 4 (1987): 25–50.

Brooke, Robert E. *Writing and Sense of Self: Identity Negotiation in Writing Workshops*. Urbana: NCTE, 1991.

Burke, Kenneth. "Literature as Equipment for Living." *The Philosophy of Literary Form*. 2nd ed. Baton Rouge: Louisiana State UP, 1967. 293–304.

——. *A Rhetoric of Motives*. Berkeley: U of California P, 1969.

——. "Terministic Screens." *Language as Symbolic Action: Essays on Life, Literature, and Method*. Berkeley: U of California P, 1966. 44–62.

Carter, Stephen. *The Culture of Disbelief: How American Law and Politics Trivialize Religious Devotion*. New York: Basic, 1993.

Chaucer, Geoffrey. *The Complete Poetry and Prose of Geoffrey Chaucer*. Ed. John H. Fisher. New York: Holt, 1977.

Cherland, Meredith. *Private Practices: Girls Reading Fiction and Constructing Identity*. London: Taylor, 1994.

Christ, Carol P. *Diving Deep and Surfacing: Women Writers on Spiritual Quest*. 2nd ed. Boston: Beacon, 1986.

Cicero. *Of Oratory*. Bizzell and Herzberg. 200–50.

Coles, William E., Jr. "Literacy for the Eighties: An Alternative to Losing." *Literacy for Life: The Demand for Reading and Writing*. Ed. Richard W. Bailey and Robin Melanie Fosheim. New York: MLA, 1983. 248–62.

Cornelius, Janet Duitsman. *"When I Can Read My Title Clear": Literacy, Slavery, and Religion in the Antebellum South*. Columbia: U of South Carolina P, 1991.

Daniell, Beth. "Composing (as) Power." *College Composition and Communication* 45 (1994): 238–46.

——. "Literacy, Politics, and Resistance: Moffett's Study of Censorship." Rev. of *Storm in the Mountains*, by James Moffett. *Journal of Teaching Writing* 7 (1988): 237–46.

——. "Narratives of Literacy: Connecting Composition to Culture." *College Composition and Communication* 50 (1999): 393–410.

———. "Ong's Great Leap: The Politics of Literacy and Orality." Diss. U of Texas at Austin, 1986.

———. Response. *College Composition and Communication* 46 (1995): 284–88.

———. "Theory, Theory Talk, and Composition." *Writing Theory and Critical Theory.* Ed. John Schilb and John Clifford. New York: MLA, 1994. 127–40.

———. "The Will to Truth: Dilemmas in Writing Research." *Against the Grain: A Volume in Honor of Maxine Hairston.* Ed. David Jolliffe, Michael Keene, Mary Trachsel, and Ralph Voss. Cresskill, NJ: Hampton, 2002. 185–95.

Dettmar, Kevin. "Iconic and Ironic Canonicity in *A Portrait.*" MLA Annual Meeting. San Francisco: 27–30 Dec. 1998.

Donehower, Kim. "The Power of Literacy: How Ordinary People Understand Literacy as a Means for Social Change." Conference on College Composition and Communication. Phoenix: 13 March 1997.

Elbow, Peter. *Writing with Power: Techniques for Mastering the Writing Process.* New York: Oxford UP, 1981.

Finders, Margaret J. *Just Girls: Hidden Literacies and Life in Junior High.* New York: Teachers College P, 1997.

Fish, Stanley. "Driving from the Letter: Truth and Indeterminacy in Milton's *Areopagitica.*" *Remembering Milton: Essays on the Texts and Traditions.* Ed. Mary Nyquist and Margaret Ferguson. New York: Methuen, 1987. 234–54.

Fishman, Andrea. *Amish Literacy: What and How It Means.* Portsmouth, NH: Heinemann, 1988.

Foehr, Regina Paxton, and Susan A. Schiller, eds. *The Spiritual Side of Writing: Releasing the Learner's Whole Potential.* Portsmouth, NH: Boynton/Cook, 1997.

Foucault, Michel. *The History of Sexuality: An Introduction.* Trans. Robert Hurley. Vol. 1. New York: Random, 1978–1980.

———. "The Order of Discourse." Bizzell and Herzberg. 1154–64.

Foucault, Michel, and Gilles Deleuze. "Intellectuals and Power: A Conversation Between Michel Foucault and Gilles Deleuze." *Language, Counter-Memory, and Practice: Selected Essays and Interviews.* Ed. and trans. Donald F. Bouchard. Ithaca: Cornell UP, 1977. 203–17.

Fox, Matthew. *Original Blessing.* Santa Fe: Bear, 1983.

Freire, Paulo. *Pedagogy of the Oppressed.* Trans. Myra Bergman Ramos. New York: Seabury, 1970.

Galtung, Johan. "Literacy, Education, and Schooling—For What?" *A Turning Point for Literacy: Adult Education for Development, the Spirit and Declaration of Persepolis: Proceedings of the International Symposium for Literacy, Persepolis, Iran.* Ed. Léon Bataille. 3–8 Sept. 1975. Oxford: Pergamon, 1976. 93–105.

Geertz, Clifford. *The Interpretation of Cultures.* New York: Basic, 1973.

Gere, Anne Ruggles. "Common Properties of Pleasure: Texts in Nineteenth Century Women's Clubs." *The Construction of Authorship: Textual Appropriation in Law and Literature*. Ed. Martha Woodmansee and Peter Jaszi. Durham: Duke UP, 1994. 383–99.

———. *Intimate Practices: Literacy and Cultural Work in U.S. Women's Clubs, 1880–1920*. Urbana: U of Illinois P, 1997.

———. "Kitchen Tables and Rented Rooms: The Extracurriculum of Composition." *College Composition and Communication* 45 (1994): 75–91.

Godzich, Wlad. Afterword. *The Postmodern Explained*. By Jean-François Lyotard. Minneapolis: U of Minnesota P, 109–36.

Goody, Jack. Introduction. *Literacy in Traditional Societies*. Ed. Jack Goody. Cambridge: Cambridge UP, 1968. 1–26.

Goody, Jack, and Ian Watt. "The Consequences of Literacy." *Comparative Studies in Society and History* 5 (1963): 304–45.

Gorgias. "Encomium of Helen." Trans. George Kennedy. *The Older Sophists*. Ed. Rosamond Kent Sprague. Columbia: U of South Carolina P, 1972. 50–54.

Graff, Harvey J. *The Legacies of Literacy: Continuities and Contradictions in Western Culture and Society*. Bloomington: Indiana UP, 1987.

Haarken, Janice. "From Al-Anon to ACOA: Codependence and the Reconstruction of Caregiving." *Signs* 18 (1993): 321–45.

Harris, Joseph. "The Idea of Community in the Study of Writing." *College Composition and Communication* 40 (1989): 11–22.

Haswell, Richard. *Gaining Ground in College Writing: Tales of Development and Interpretation*. Dallas: Southern Methodist UP, 1991.

———. "Old posts on research." E-mail to the author. 15 Mar. 2000. Originally posted <wpa-l@asuvm.irne.asu.edu> 8 Mar. 2000.

Havelock, Eric. *Preface to Plato*. Cambridge: Harvard UP, 1963.

Heath, Shirley Brice. "Protean Shapes in Literacy Events: Ever-Shifting Oral and Literate Traditions." *Spoken and Written Language: Exploring Orality and Literacy*. Ed. Deborah Tannen. Norwood, NJ: Ablex, 1982. 91–117.

———. *Ways with Words: Language, Life, and Work in Communities and Classrooms*. Cambridge: Cambridge UP, 1983.

Herrington, Anne J., and Marcia Curtis. *Persons in Progress: Four Stories of Writing and Personal Development in College*. Urbana: NCTE, 2000.

Hirsch, E. D., Jr. *Cultural Literacy: What Every American Needs To Know*. Boston: Houghton, 1987.

Holland, Norman. *5 Readers Reading*. New Haven: Yale UP, 1975.

———. "Unity Identity Text Self." *Reader-Response Criticism: From Formalism to Post-Structuralism*. Ed. Jane Tompkins. Baltimore: Johns Hopkins UP, 1980. 118–33.

Holzman, Michael. "The Social Context of Literacy Education." *College English* 48 (1986): 27–33.

hooks, bell. *Sisters of the Yam: Black Women and Self-Recovery*. Boston: South End, 1993.

———. *Talking Back: Thinking Feminist, Thinking Black.* Boston: South End, 1989.

Horsman, Jennifer. *Something in My Mind Besides the Everyday: Women and Literacy.* Toronto: Women's, 1990.

Howard, Richard. A Note on the Text. *The Pleasure of the Text.* By Roland Barthes. Trans. Richard Miller, New York: Hill, 1975. v–viii.

"Inside Al-Anon: 'So for Unity's Sake . . .'" *Forum: The International Monthly Journal of Al-Anon* 48.7 (July 1999): 18–22.

Isocrates. *Antidosis. Isocrates in Three Volumes.* Trans. George Norlin. 1929. Vol. 2. Loeb Classical Library. Cambridge: Harvard UP, 1982. 181–365.

Ives, Edward D. *The Tape-Recorded Interview: A Manual for Field Workers in Folklore and Oral History.* Knoxville: U of Tennessee P, 1974.

Jensen, George H. *Storytelling in Alcoholics Anonymous: A Rhetorical Analysis.* Carbondale: Southern Illinois UP, 2000.

Kaminer, Wendy. *I'm Dysfunctional, You're Dysfunctional: The Recovery Movement and Other Self-Help Fashions.* New York: Addison-Wesley, 1992. New York: Random, 1993.

Kapitzke, Cushla. *Literacy and Religion: The Textual Politics and Practice of Seventh-Day Adventism.* Studies in Written Language and Literacy. Amsterdam: Benjamins, 1995.

King, Stephen. "Why We Crave Horror Movies." *Reading Culture.* 2nd ed. Ed. Diana George and John Trimbur. New York: Harper, 1995. 357–59. Rpt. of *Playboy* Jan. 1981: 150+.

Kirsch, Gesa E., and Joy S. Ritchie. "Beyond the Personal: Theorizing a Politics of Location in Composition Research." *College Composition and Communication* 46 (1995): 7–29.

Kurtz, Ernest. *Not-God: A History of Alcoholics Anonymous.* Center City, MN: Hazelden, 1979.

Kurtz, Ernest, and Katherine Ketcham. *The Spirituality of Imperfection: Storytelling and the Journey to Wholeness.* New York: Bantam, 1992.

Lester, Toby. "Oh, Gods!" *Atlantic Monthly.* Feb. 2002: 37–45.

Lorde, Audre. "The Transformation of Silence into Language and Action." *Sister Outsider: Essays and Speeches.* Freedom, CA: Crossing, 1984. 40–44.

Lyotard, Jean-François. *The Postmodern Condition: A Report on Knowledge.* Trans. Geoff Bennington and Brian Massumi. Minneapolis: U of Minnesota P, 1984.

MacNealy, Mary Sue. *Strategies for Empirical Research in Writing.* Boston: Allyn, 1999.

Miller, Jean Baker. *Toward a New Psychology of Women.* Boston: Beacon, 1976.

Miller, Jean Baker, and Irene Pierce Stiver. *The Healing Connection: How Women Form Relationships in Therapy and in Life.* Boston: Beacon, 1997.

Moffett, James. *Storm in the Mountains: A Case Study of Censorship, Conflict, and Consciousness.* Carbondale: Southern Illinois UP, 1988.

Morgan, Dan. "Ethical Issues Raised by Students' Personal Writing." *College English* 60 (1998): 318–25.

Morrissey, Lee. Guest Lecture. English 801. Clemson University, Clemson, SC. 15 Mar. 2000.

Mortensen, Peter, and Gesa E. Kirsch. Introduction. *Ethics and Representation in Qualitative Studies of Literacy.* Ed. Peter Mortensen and Gesa E. Kirsch. Urbana: NCTE, 1996. xix–xxxiv.

Moss, Beverly J. "The Black Sermon as Literacy Event." Diss. U of Illinois at Chicago, 1988.

———. "Creating a Community: Literacy in African-American Churches." *Literacy Across Communities.* Ed. Beverly J. Moss. Cresskill, NJ: Hampton, 1994. 147–78.

Newkirk, Thomas. "The Narrative Roots of Case Study." *Methods and Methodology in Composition Research.* Ed. Gesa E. Kirsch and Patricia A. Sullivan. Carbondale: Southern Illinois UP, 1992. 130–52.

Oakley, Ann. "Interviewing Women: A Contradiction in Terms." *Doing Feminist Research.* Ed. Helen Roberts. London: Routledge, 1981. 30–61.

Olsen, Tillie. *Silences.* New York: Delacorte, 1978.

Olson, David R. "From Utterance to Text: The Bias of Language in Speech and Writing." *Harvard Educational Review* 47 (1977): 257–81.

Ong, Walter J., Jr. *Orality and Literacy: The Technologizing of the Word.* London: Methuen, 1982.

O'Reilly, Edmund B. *Sobering Tales: Narratives of Alcoholism and Recovery.* Amherst: U of Massachusetts P, 1997.

Oxenham, John. *Literacy: Writing, Reading, and Social Organisation.* London: Routledge, 1980.

Peck, M. Scott. *The Road Less Traveled: A New Psychology of Love, Traditional Values, and Spiritual Growth.* New York: Simon, 1978.

Pennebaker, James W. *Opening Up: The Healing Power of Confiding in Others.* New York: Morrow, 1990. New York: Avon, 1991.

———. "Self-Expressive Writing: Implications for Health, Education, and Welfare." *Nothing Begins With N: New Investigations of Freewriting.* Ed. Pat Belanoff, Peter Elbow, and Sheryl Fontaine. Carbondale: Southern Illinois UP, 1991. 157–69.

Perelman, Chaim. *The Realm of Rhetoric.* Trans. William Kluback. Notre Dame: U of Notre Dame P, 1982.

Perelman, Chaim, and Lucie Olbrechts-Tyteca. *The New Rhetoric: A Treatise on Argumentation.* Trans. John Wilkinson and Purcell Weaver. Notre Dame: U of Notre Dame P, 1969.

Perfetti, Charles A. "Language, Speech, and Print: Some Asymmetries in the Acquisition of Literacy." *Comprehending Oral and Written Language.* Ed. Rosalind Horowitz and S. Jay Samuels. San Diego: Academic, 1987. 355–69.

Radway, Janice A. *Reading the Romance: Women, Patriarchy, and Popular Litera-ture*. Chapel Hill: U of North Caroline P, 1984.

Resnick, Daniel P., and Lauren B. Resnick. "The Nature of Literacy: An Histori-cal Exploration." *Harvard Educational Review* 47 (1977): 370–85.

Robertson, Nan. *Getting Better: Inside Alcoholics Anonymous*. New York: Morrow, 1988.

Rosenblatt, Louise M. *The Reader, the Text, the Poem: The Transactional Theory of the Literary Work*. Carbondale: Southern Illinois UP, 1978.

Scribner, Sylvia. "Literacy in Three Metaphors." *Perspectives on Literacy*. Ed. Eugene Kintgen, Barry Kroll, and Mike Rose. Carbondale: Southern Illi-nois UP, 1988. 71–81. Rpt. of *American Journal of Education* 93 (1984): 5–21.

Scribner, Sylvia, and Michael Cole. "Unpackaging Literacy." Kintgen, Kroll, and Rose. 57–70.

Selfe, Cynthia L. *Technology and Literacy in the Twenty-First Century: The Impor-tance of Paying Attention*. Studies in Writing & Rhetoric. Carbondale: Southern Illinois UP, 1999.

Sicherman, Barbara. "Sense and Sensibility: A Case Study of Women's Reading in Late-Victorian America." *Reading in America: Literature and Social His-tory*. Ed. Cathy N. Davidson. Baltimore: Johns Hopkins UP, 1989. 201–25.

Simonds, Wendy. *Women and Self-Help Culture: Reading Between the Lines*. New Brunswick, NJ: Rutgers UP, 1992.

Smith, Dorothy E. "Telling the Truth after Postmodernism." *Writing the Social: Critique, Theory, and Investigations*. Toronto: U of Toronto P, 1999. 96–130.

Sommers, Nancy. "Learning to Write Within a Discipline." Conference on Col-lege Composition and Communication, Denver. 15 Mar. 2001.

Street, Brian V. *Literacy in Theory and Practice*. Cambridge UP, 1984.

———. *Social Literacies: Critical Approaches to Literacy in Development, Ethnog-raphy, and Education*. London: Longman, 1995.

Swearingen, C. Jan. *Rhetoric and Irony: Western Literacy and Western Lies*. New York: Oxford UP, 1991.

Trachsel, Mary. "Horse Stories and Romance Fiction: Variants or Alternative Texts of Female Identity." *Reader* 38–39 (Fall/Spring 1997–98): 20–41.

Trimbur, John. "Composition Studies: Postmodern or Popular." *Into the Field: Sites of Composition Studies*. Ed. Anne Ruggles Gere. New York: MLA, 1993. 117–32.

Ulanov, Ann, and Barry Ulanov. *Primary Speech: A Psychology of Prayer*. Atlanta: Knox, 1982.

Walters, Keith. "Not-So-Hidden Literacy in an Unprogrammed Quaker Meet-ing." MLA Responsibilities for Literacy Conference. Pittsburgh. Sep. 1990.

West, Cornel. "Nihilism in Black America." *Race Matters*. Boston: Beacon, 1993. 11–20.

Index

souls of, 15, 75, 135, 145; stories of, 15, 36
World Service Conference of Al-Anon, 11, 69, 89
writing (*see also* genres of writing): benefits of, 61; to clarify values, 156; as confession (*see also* Fourth Step), 40–41, 48, 50, 52–53, 59, 74, 133, 163–64; dangers of, 161; "Dear God letters" (*see also* genres of writing, letters), 39, 54–55, 57–58, 63, 134; to define identity, 156; domestic function of, 59; empirical studies of, 155–56; essays (*see* genres of writing); expressive, 44, 163; fiction, 70; Fourth Step and, 40–41, 59, 133; "God Can notes" (*see* genres of writing); honesty and, 44–45; ideology of school, 70,

112, 162–64; journals (*see* genres of writing); letters (*see* genres of writing); and notebook, 54, 60, 68; notes to self, 59; permanence of, 62, 134; poetry (*see* poetry); proofreading, 69; prose (*see* prose); reaction paper (*see* genres of writing); as record, 58, 61–63, 131, 134; school-sponsored, 141–42, 158, 162; self-examination and, 44, 51, 66, 74, 151; "spiral notebook," 54, 60–61, 68, 134; spoken, made verbal, 72; steno pad, 54, 58, 70; as "symptom of group membership," 65–66; talking and, 2, 17, 23, 47–48, 50–51, 75–76, 132, 134; to work through problems, 156; and written form (*see also* genres of writing), 44, 54, 63

BETH DANIELL is an associate professor in the Department of English at Clemson University, where she has served as the director of composition and as the director of undergraduate studies. She teaches a variety of courses, including first-year composition, women's studies, ethnic literature, modern rhetoric, and classical rhetoric. At the graduate level, she teaches seminars in literacy, rhetoric, and composition theory.

Studies in Writing & Rhetoric

In 1980 the Conference on College Composition and Communication established the Studies in Writing & Rhetoric (SWR) series as a forum for monograph-length arguments or presentations that engage general compositionists. SWR encourages extended essays or research reports addressing any issue in composition and rhetoric from any theoretical or research perspective as long as the general significance to the field is clear. Previous SWR publications serve as models for prospective authors; in addition, contributors may propose alternate formats and agendas that inform or extend the field's current debates.

SWR is particularly interested in projects that connect the specific research site or theoretical framework to contemporary classroom and institutional contexts of direct concern to compositionists across the nation. Such connections may come from several approaches, including cultural, theoretical, field-based, gendered, historical, and interdisciplinary. SWR especially encourages monographs by scholars early in their careers, by established scholars who wish to share an insight or exhortation with the field, and by scholars of color.

The SWR series editor and editorial board members are committed to working closely with prospective authors and offering significant developmental advice for encouraged manuscripts and prospectuses. Editorships rotate every five years. Prospective authors intending to submit a prospectus during the 2002 to 2007 editorial appointment should obtain submission guidelines from Robert Brooke, SWR editor, University of Nebraska-Lincoln, Department of English, P.O. Box 880337, 202 Andrews Hall, Lincoln, NE 68588-0337.

General inquiries may also be addressed to Sponsoring Editor, Studies in Writing & Rhetoric, Southern Illinois University Press, P.O. Box 3697, Carbondale, IL 62902-3697.